Made Over

Renewal from the Inside Out

Dr. Brenda J. Robinson

xulon PRESS

Made Over
by Dr. Brenda J. Robinson

Printed in the United States of America

ISBN 1-59781-884-4

Unless otherwise indicated, Bible quotations are taken from the King James Version Bible.

www.xulonpress.com

Table of Contents

Foreword vii

Acknowledgements ix

Chapter 1   Looking in the Mirror............11

Chapter 2   Facing the Facts...................41

Chapter 3   Dealing with Reality............57

Chapter 4   Transforming the Mind.........75

Chapter 5   Reviving the Heart................91

Chapter 6   Nursing the Wounds............105

Chapter 7   Overcoming the Pain...........119

Chapter 8   The Healing Process.............137

Chapter 9   The Unveiling.....................155

Chapter 10   Made Over...........................173

Foreword

Made Over

I've discovered through many years of ministry work that most every Christian struggles with insecurities, the past, fear, rebellion and the effects of sin. These struggles drastically impair the confidence and courage of God's people. They cause our faith in God to waver, and we find ourselves broken and tattered.

This was my life once. My brokenness brought me to a point of low self-esteem and worthlessness. I appeared to be strong on the outside, but inside I was withered and dying. My faith in God had vanished. I doubted every truth and blessing God sent my way. I could not believe that God loved me.

I began to realize that something had to change, and I knew it would have to change from the inside out. I knew my heart would have to be cleansed and softened, but I didn't know where to start. The only hope I had was in asking God to change my life. I had just enough sense to know that God was the answer, but I feared that I was too far gone even for His grace.

God did not hesitate to respond to my call for help. He began a renovation process in my life. He readjusted my thinking. He revealed His unconditional love, and I fell in love with Him. God did a complete, extreme makeover in every area of my life.

Eventually, the inward makeover became outwardly noticeable. I began to share the transforming power of God with others who were struggling with the same situations I had faced. My passion for sharing the healing powers of the Great Physician became my ultimate goal. I knew God could work in anyone's life since He had done such a great transformation in mine. No one is beyond hope in Him.

God wants to do a makeover starting with those things that are deeply hidden, those things we don't want anyone else to know about. He wants to deal with the things we refuse to talk about, confront or deal with. The Great Physician will remove the things that have caused us grief and the things that Satan uses against us.

I first shared these truths before 1200 women at a women's conference. I dealt with those hidden issues that hinder our walk with God, and I watched the holy presence of God purge and repair the broken hearts of women who were living in defeat and depression. I witnessed extreme makeovers taking place right before my eyes. I watched frowns turn to smiles as tears began to flow from the emotional releases. I witnessed spiritual revival take place as God's truths were brought to light. I rejoiced as lost souls were made alive through salvation. God's transforming power was evident in both young and old. Throughout the building, the tough exteriors were breaking down to reveal women being made over for God's glory and their good.

It seemed that I was in the Potter's house, watching Him crush the damaged pieces and make them over as vessels of honor. The wheel turned steadily as His hands removed the impurities in these pieces of clay. Once each piece was finished, His love for each woman was revealed and those women all walked away with a makeover unlike any other. Lives were permanently transformed in holiness, and the effects are still talked about today.

No make-up was involved. We didn't do any facials. Not one tube of lipstick was used in that conference. No fashion show or fine apparel was presented, but God's radiant beauty and righteousness shone upon each face as hearts were released from bondage. Everyone there left looking like a bride on her wedding day, waiting for her Groom to appear.

My prayer is that this book will capture your heart as it did the hearts of those women and girls present at the conference. Prepare yourself for the spiritual change that God wants to perform in your life. Your relationship with God is about to be made over.

Acknowledgements

This book is dedicated to my son Kevin Robinson for his willingness to support his parents in the service God has called us to do. Kevin, I love you and appreciate your love. You bring great joy to our lives. You may not travel with us on the road and you may not sing on stage but you truly are our support system. Thank you for believing in what we do.

It is an absolute joy to serve Jesus Christ. It is an even greater joy to serve Him with the precious family and staff that He has blessed me with. I know I have the greatest husband, children, daughter-in-law and grandchild in the whole world. God hand picked each one of them just for me. I praise God from whom all blessings flow.

I want to thank my husband and my children for always being there for me even when I am stressed from deadlines and burnout. You guys are the best. Your unconditional love is amazing. I am so proud of all of you.

I want to thank Karen Tinsley my personal assistant for all her hard work on every book I have ever written. Karen, you are a blessing. I praise God for you every day.

Debra, you may be my sister but you are the greatest encourager any sister could ever ask for. Thank you for all you do for me. There is not space enough to list all the times you have cheered me on when I was tired and ready to give up. I know God has that list in Heaven. You are very special to me and I love you with all my heart.

Chapter 1

Looking in the Mirror

James 1:23-24: *"For if any be a hearer of the word, and not a doer, he is like unto a man beholding his natural face in a glass: ²⁴For he beholdeth himself, and goeth his way, and straightway forgetteth what manner of man he was."*

Mirrors! They tell the truth. Each time I look into one, I see all of my flaws. I see lines, wrinkles, crow's feet and scars. I immediately start thinking: What can I do to stop the aging process? Then I realize that I should have done something years ago to slow this process down. I should have been using moisturizers, night creams, cucumbers or Preparation H (which I could have sworn was made for a different purpose!). In our desperation, we will resort to extreme makeover options.

The truth is, when we look in the mirror, we don't just look at the face. We view the whole body. The longer we look, the worse we feel about ourselves. We remember the times we vowed to start taking precautions against aging, and we remember that we never took those precautions. Now, we are left to mask the flaws, blemishes, lines and wrinkles. We cover them over because we were hearers and not doers. We were all talk and no action.

"You can be made over by the Great Physician."

Our Christian lives are basically in the same condition. We have talked about a deeper relationship with God, but we are still beholding our natural face. We have neither made changes nor taken precautions to keep ourselves pleasing to God. We are faithful to hear the Word, but we fail to do the Word. We go our own way instead of going God's way. The process of disobedience ages us quickly. We see its effects each time we look in the mirror. We tend to mask what we see in the mirror with excuses and denial. We find ourselves in critical condition, and the enemy convinces us there is no hope for renewal.

I am here to tell you that you can be made over by the Great Physician. He will renew you from the inside out. His mirror reflects newness and hope. It does not lie. Let's start the process of a makeover with Jesus Christ. I am certain you will love what you see when the process is complete.

The makeover will be painful, but the finished product will be worth it all. This makeover will force you to make a break from the past so that you can never go back to it. It will make you free from the bondages of life. It will prepare you to radiate the love of Christ.

This extreme makeover will require you to:

- Deal with the past
- Face the present
- Prepare for the future
- Complete the work

Shall we get started? Let the makeover begin!

Day 1   *Dealing with the Past*

Ephesians 4:22-27 *"That ye put off concerning the former conversation the old man, which is corrupt according to the deceitful lusts;* [23]*And be renewed in the spirit of your mind;* [24]*And that ye put on the new man, which after God is created in righteousness and true holiness.* [25]*Wherefore putting away lying, speak every man truth with his neighbour: for we are members one of another.* [26]*Be ye angry, and sin not: let not the sun go down upon your wrath:* [27]*Neither give place to the devil."*

Makeovers! Why do we feel that we need extreme makeovers? Most of the time, we feel this need because we are stuck in our pasts. We forget to put off the old man and be renewed in the spirit of our minds because of the things done in our pasts. We all know that Satan's warfare is raged in our minds, convincing us that we can neither escape our past nor be satisfied and content with who we are now in Christ. We must understand that if we have received Jesus Christ as our Savior, we have the power to put off or take off the former conversation (lifestyle/behavior) of our old man who is corrupt.

Our past is not the only adversary that makes us feel that we need extreme makeovers. We have adversaries that deceive our minds and control our thinking. This is why our scripture text teaches us to "be renewed in the spirit of our minds." The word "renewed" here literally means to be "made new." When we received Jesus as our Savior, He made us new on the inside. However, the outside and the mind has to be made new on a daily basis. The outside and the mind are controlled by our flesh. It is imperative that once we are settled into our position as Christians, we must set up daily appointments for renewing our minds.

The reason we need extreme makeovers is we are not satisfied with our lifestyles, ourselves or our circumstances. We can usually relate these dissatisfactions back to our past.

We want to have the lifestyles of the rich and famous. We want to be like others, have what others have, and do what others do. We strive to be accepted in the world. Thus, we create for ourselves a life of peer pressure and problems. We are smothered by the former things.

What lifestyle choices have you made in the past that still control your life? __

_____

How has it affected your relationship with God? _____

_____

Has it affected your confidence as a Christian? _____

_____

How often are you reminded of these lifestyle decisions? _____

_____

Who reminds you of your past? Your church, your spouse, your friend, family, co-workers, etc. _____

_____

The next subject that we must deal with is the dissatisfaction with ourselves. This is where we stand in front of a mirror and find everything wrong with our appearance. We start making a file of everything we want to makeover. "A new nose would be great maybe a lip job, liposuction, or a tummy tuck might be better. I could color my hair or get a brow lift. My ears are too big; my face is too fat. I need to lose weight. I need to put some weight on." That's right! There are some out there who even battle with underweight problems. The problem with being satisfied with ourselves once again relates to our past. Someone has verbally abused us and criticized our appearance. Perhaps it could be from the way we were raised or the rejection of others while growing up.

"The one who constantly reminds us of our past has absolutely no future."

Appearance is not the only enemy of "ourselves." We also have the lack of self-esteem, no confidence, unworthiness, or lack of education. We also battle issues of being accepted by others and doing whatever it takes to fit in with the crowd. These issues are the scars of the past that plague our minds every day. The enemy wreaks havoc in our lives because of our "self" issues. He is a reminder of our wrong decisions, faults, failures and mistakes. We must remember, the one who constantly reminds us of our past has absolutely no future. Satan's final destination is hell. As a born again child of God your destination is Heaven forever. This is why our scripture text teaches us to…"put on the new man, which after God is created in righteousness and true holiness." Therefore, as we look at "ourselves" from the inside out instead of the outside in, we will find ourselves to be "in Christ".

Colossians 3:1-13 says:

> "If ye then be risen with Christ, seek those things which are above, where Christ sitteth on the right hand of God. [2]Set your affection on things above, not on things on the earth. [3]For ye are dead, and your life is hid with Christ in God. [4]When Christ, who is our life, shall appear, then shall ye also appear with him in glory.[5]Mortify therefore your members which are upon the earth; fornication, uncleanness, inordinate affection, evil concupiscence, and covetousness, which is idolatry: [6]For which

things' sake the wrath of God cometh on the children of disobedience: [7]In the which ye also walked some time, when ye lived in them. [8]But now ye also put off all these; anger, wrath, malice, blasphemy, filthy communication out of your mouth. [9]Lie not one to another, seeing that ye have put off the old man with his deeds; [10]And have put on the new man, which is renewed in knowledge after the image of him that created him: [11]Where there is neither Greek nor Jew, circumcision nor uncircumcision, Barbarian, Scythian, bond nor free: but Christ is all, and in all. [12]Put on therefore, as the elect of God, holy and beloved, bowels of mercies, kindness, humbleness of mind, meekness, longsuffering; [13]Forbearing one another, and forgiving one another, if any man have a quarrel against any: even as Christ forgave you, so also do ye."

Before we can find self satisfaction we will have to switch mirrors. The mirror we look in speaks to and about our flesh. God's mirror (His word) speaks about His righteousness becoming our righteousness. This fact alone can deliver us from the bondage of bad decisions. Through the eyes of God He sees our potential, not our past. This is why Colossians 3:5-8 says, "Mortify therefore your members which are upon the earth; fornication, uncleanness, inordinate affection, evil concupiscence, and covetousness, which is idolatry: [6]For which things' sake the wrath of God cometh on the children of disobedience: [7]In the which ye also walked some time, when ye lived in them. [8]But now ye also put off all these; anger, wrath, malice, blasphemy, filthy communication out of your mouth."

We are commanded here that dissatisfaction with ourselves is wrong. If we take it to the extreme of dwelling in it we will feel inadequate and unworthy. God knows who we are and everything about our past. We are the only ones who keep a file.

What part of the past is still controlling how you feel about yourself? _____

_____

What part of your past is standing between you and God?_____

_____

What part of your past is Satan reminding you of daily? _____

_____

What part of your past do you feel that God just will not forgive you for? ___

An extreme makeover requires self-examination. Tomorrow we'll examine our condition based on the effect our past has had on us.

Daily Reflections: Your Thoughts on Today's Study

_____

_____

_____

_____

_____

_____

_____

Prayer Journal: Your Prayer on Today's Study

_____

_____

_____

_____

_____

_____

_____

Day 2   *Self-Examination*

Psalm 26:2: *"Examine me, O LORD, and prove me; try my reins and my heart."*

Do any of these questions sound familiar to you? Really think about it and be honest with yourself, because honesty makes a pure heart.

- ☐ Why can't I live for God the way I'm supposed to?
- ☐ Why do I let all of these other things sidetrack me?
- ☐ Why can't I understand the Bible when I read it?
- ☐ Why doesn't God ever answer my prayers?
- ☐ Why do I keep going back to the things that cause sin in my life?
- ☐ Why do I keep putting myself in bondage?
- ☐ If I'm so miserable with my life, why can't I let God have full control?

I am so thankful that God saw fit to answer all these questions for me. He will answer them for you, too, if you are seeking. Don't be ashamed to answer these questions honestly. Being honest with yourself is the first step toward spiritual growth. Jesus taught us the significance of honesty in Luke 8:15. He said, "But that on the good ground are they, which in an honest and good heart, having heard the word, keep it, and bring forth fruit with patience." In this Scripture we see that it takes being honest with ourselves and with God to become victorious, effective Christians.

"Being honest with yourself is the first step toward spiritual growth."

Examining Our Condition

Lamentations 3:40 says, "Let us search and try our ways, and turn again to the Lord." Let's study the first part of this verse and apply it to our lives. The verse starts with, "Let us search and try our ways." The Hebrew "ways," in this specific passage, means a course of life or mode of action. The first part of Lamentations 3:40 tells us that we must examine our way of life in order to truly see our condition in Christ.

The list of words below is a list of the symptoms of our condition. Which of these represents your way of life for Christ? Check the ones that you think apply to you:

- ☐ Hindered - Galatians 5:7.
- ☐ Hungry - Mark 2:23-28.
- ☐ Desiring Him - Psalm 37:4-5.

□ Unfaithful – 1 Corinthians 4:1-2.
□ Frustrated - Galatians 2:20-21.
□ Angry - Psalm 37:8 & Matthew 5:22-24.
□ Bitter - Ephesians 4:31.
□ Afraid - Living in or with fear. 1 John 4:18.
□ Distressed - Psalm 120:1-2.
□ Weary - Isaiah 40:31.
□ Discontent - 1 Samuel 22:2 and Psalm 107:9.
□ Content - Hebrews 13:5.
□ Discouraged - Psalm 27:1-14.
□ Unsaved/Lost - Romans 10:13; Luke 5:32, 19:10.
□ Confused - 1 Corinthians 14:33 and James 1:5.
□ Lukewarm - Revelation 2:4, 3:16, and Psalm 44:20-21.
□ Unstable - James 1:8, and 2 Peter 3:16.

If you did check one or more of these items, you have just learned how to apply the first part of Lamentations 3:40 to your life. You are on your way to becoming a more pleasing child of God. You have just admitted to yourself and God that your way of life is ready for a makeover through Him.

Now that we have examined and confessed our way of life in Christ Jesus, we are ready to tackle the second part of Lamentations 3:40. It says, "Turn again to the Lord." Some of you are saying by now, "Well, how can I turn to the Lord after all those items I had to check? Why, He's not going to give me the time of the day after that. I'm a hopeless case!" Well, listen. Its okay for you to feel that way because you have just realized your condition in Jesus, and that is what He wants you to see about yourself. Now you must confess your faults to Him, trust in Him to take care of them, and be patient while He's doing it. When you have done this, you have applied the second part of Lamentations 3:40 to your life.

We are now ready to deal with our past. I mean deal with everything, from A-Z, leaving nothing out. We're even dealing with the most recent past issues.

Yesterday is now the past. This morning is now the past. We are going to deal with it all. There are three principles to dealing with our past. Let's cover them carefully:

1. Confront the past

Ephesians 2:2-5: Wherein in time past ye walked according to the course of this world, according to the prince of the power of the air, the spirit that now worketh in the children of disobedience: [3]Among whom also we all had our conversation in times past in the lusts of our flesh, fulfilling the desires of the flesh and of the mind; and were by nature the children of wrath, even as others. [4]But God, who is rich in mercy, for his great love wherewith he loved us, [5]Even when we were dead in sins, hath quickened us together with Christ, (by grace ye are saved;)

Who?

- ✔ What?
- ✔ When?
- ✔ Where?
- ✔ Why?
- ✔ How long has it been?
- ✔ How does it make you feel?
- ✔ Are you dwelling in it?
- ✔ Do you want to deal with it?

As we confront our past the enemy has to flee. The mind begins to clear so that God can do the transforming.

Song of Solomon 2:11-13: "For, lo, the winter is past, the rain is over and gone; [12]The flowers appear on the earth; the time of the singing of birds is come, and the voice of the turtle is heard in our land; [13]The fig tree putteth forth her green figs, and the vines with the tender grape give a good smell. Arise, my love, my fair one, and come away."

2. Confess the past.

1 John 1:7-9: "But if we walk in the light, as he is in the light, we have fellowship one with another, and the blood of Jesus Christ his Son cleanseth us from all sin. [8]If we say that we have no sin, we deceive ourselves, and the truth is not in us. [9]If we confess our sins, he is faithful and just to forgive us our sins, and to cleanse us from all unrighteousness."

- ✔ What is in your file that you keep pulling up?
- ✔ Are you still active in it today?
- ✔ Is it hindering you from serving the Lord?
- ✔ Which of the following categories does your past fall under? Circle the appropriate word(s).

Sin	Sorrow	Grief
Disappointment	Shattered expectations	Failures
Mistakes	Lust of the flesh	Lust of the world
Addictions	Adultery	Fornication
Idolatry	Anger	Rebellion
Fear	Regret	Unforgiveness
Hatred	Other	

Confession is admitting this is who I am and this is what I've done. Once confession takes place freedom from the past begins to develop not only in your mind but also in your hearts.

3. Conquer the past.

Romans 8:37: "Nay, in all these things we are more than conquerors through him that loved us."

- ✔ Confess it to God
- ✔ Take it off and put on the new man
- ✔ Leave it behind
- ✔ Transform the mind
- ✔ Forgive yourself and others involved
- ✔ Deal with it do not dwell in it
- ✔ Attack your past with the Word of God
    - ✔ Believe God's mind about your past (your sins and iniquities I remember no more)
    - ✔ Refuse the enemies lies
    - ✔ Destroy the file

Second Corinthians 5:17: "Therefore if any man be in Christ, he is a new creature: old things are passed away; behold, all things are become new."

Page after page in the Word of God reveals people whose lives were affected by their past. Many Bible personalities were influenced by the circumstances of their past:

> Dysfunction = The woman at the well
> Sinfulness = Rahab
> Evil = Jezebel
> Emotional instability = Martha
> Abuse = physical, verbal, and/or sexual - Tamar
> Worldly = Miriam
> Deceptive = Delilah
> Sexual promiscuity = Gomer

The effects of the past can and will control everything about our lives if we allow them to have that control. However, as children of God we have been made free from the bondage of our past. It is time that we not only destroy our past but also bury it in the sea of forgetfulness.

Your past has been painful and devastating for you. There will always be reminders of your past, but starting right now we can take those reminders and turn them from negatives to positives. Romans 8:28 says, "And we know that all things work together for good to them that love God, to them who are the called according to his purpose."

Let's start right now finding the positives in our past.

1. God protected you.
2. God made a way of escape.

3. You learned more about God through it.
4. God does not remind you of it.
5. It humbled you.
6. God is over your past; shouldn't you be?
7. It did not take your life.
8. God loves you in spite of your past.
9. God will use it for His glory.
10. God does not blame you, and He is not ashamed of you because of your past.

I really think that we truly have covered everything from A-Z concerning our past (see Appendix A at end of the book). We can rejoice in the fact that God cares so much about our feelings. He cares about how the past consumes and controls our thoughts and our actions.

God's heart is to free you of your past once and for all. The darkness of your past must be conquered right now through faith in Jesus Christ and the work that He did at Calvary for your freedom. I John 2:8 says, "Again, a new commandment I write unto you, which thing is true in him and in you: because the darkness is past, and the true light now shineth." Regardless of your past, the truth is, it is over. You do not have to keep living in the darkness. Christ is the true light that now shines within you.

We have confronted, confessed, and conquered our past in this session. These principles will only hold up if you:

1. Trust God's Word
2. Surrender to God
3. Destroy your file

"God's heart is to free you of your past once and for all."

Are you here to destroy and get past your past once and for all? I pray that you have come to live in freedom from your past. God has come with one final word for you about your past. Do you want to know what he has to say? He has brought you here to speak to you. He knows everything about you from A-Z. He knows your life. He knows right now that one specific thing that constantly grieves your heart and makes you feel that you are unforgivable, undeserving, unwanted, unaccepted, unworthy and unprofitable.

All of these feelings are from Satan, your flesh and the world. God is the opposite of all of these things. He is forgiving and forgetting. To Him you are deserving, wanted, accepted, worthy and profitable.

Daily Reflections: *Your Thoughts on Today's Study*

_____

_____

_____

_____

_____

_____

_____

_____

Prayer Journal: *Your Prayer on Today's Study*

_____

_____

_____

_____

_____

_____

_____

Day 3 *Facing the Present*

Psalm 46:1: *"God is our refuge and strength, a very present help in trouble."*

We face life everyday wondering if it will ever work out. It seems that we give life our all, yet we find ourselves discontent, distraught, and doubtful that life is going to get any better. We wonder, "Does God really care?"

Most of us know that Jesus is our Savior, and we strive to please Him. But, it seems the closer we draw to Him the harder life gets. Our scripture text teaches us that, regardless of our present circumstances, "God is our refuge and strength, a very present help in trouble."

With this promise, God is calling us into an extreme makeover for our present circumstances. Without God's help we will drown ourselves in doubt. Satan will lie to us, trying to convince us that our present problems are too far gone or too unimportant for God to intervene. This lie of the devil is contradicted in Romans 8:18, 31. Verse 18 says, "For I reckon that the sufferings of this present time are not worthy to be compared with the glory which shall be revealed in us." Verse 31 says, "What shall we then say to these things? If God be for us, who can be against us?"

With these truths before us, we must face the present and allow the Lord to make our lives over. Let's face the moment, the problems, and then praise Him for His blessings. Let's confess the present challenges while we identify the culprit.

Let's answer these questions one at a time:

1. What are my problems? _____
   _____

2. When will it get better? _____
   _____

3. What are my spiritual responsibilities? _____
   _____

4. Why am I here?_____
   _____

5. How do I deal with this?_____
   _____

6. Who is to blame? _____
   _____

As we face and search for the answers to these questions we must remember that the same God who has conquered our past is the same God who controls the present. Galatians 1:3-4 says, "Grace be to you and peace from God the Father, and from our Lord Jesus Christ, [4]Who gave himself for our sins, that he might deliver us from this present evil world, according to the will of God and our Father."

1. What are my present problems? Marriage, Children, Job, Money, Depression, Physical, Spiritual, Intentional sin, Recurring sin, Church, Relationships, Other

2. When will it get better? When you seek God's advice, When you apply God's truth, When you accept God's solution, When you obey God's instruction, When you turn it over to God completely, When you place your faith in God, When you stop trying to control it, When the lesson has been learned.

"God who has conquered our past is the same God who controls the present."

3. What are my spiritual responsibilities? Pray to God, Study about Him, Worship Him, Praise Him, Trust Him, Abide in Him.

4. Why am I here? God wants to teach you, God wants you to learn of Him, God wants to use you through this, God is making you an example, God is maturing you.

5. How do I deal with this? Seek God's mind on the matter, Wait for God's instruction, Serve God in the midst of it, Trust that God knows best, Communicate the problem with someone you trust, Allow God to deal with it.

6. Who is to blame? Satan, The flesh, The world

God is never at fault when we think that things are topsy turvey. When we blame things on God, we are responding from the flesh and the desire to just be rescued.

God doesn't want to do makeovers only in us. He also wants to do makeovers in our churches, our marriages, our children, our home, our families, and in other areas that He knows needs some spiritual adjustments. In order for these adjustments to be made we will have to start today, this present moment, fulfilling the responsibilities of our spiritual condition. Titus 2:11-13 instructs us like this: "For the grace of God that bringeth salvation hath appeared to all men, [12]Teaching us that, denying ungodliness and worldly lusts, we should live soberly, righteously, and godly, in this present world; [13]Looking for that blessed hope, and the glorious appearing of the great God and our Saviour Jesus Christ."

The responsibilities of our spiritual condition are:

1. Prayer
2. Faith
3. Study
4. Obedience

When we do our part, the Holy Spirit is able to counteract the evils of the devil and the flesh. These are not only our responsibilities; they are also our resources and our pathway to a beautiful walk and relationship with our precious Savior.

1. Prayer

Our first responsibility is to have a dedicated, unhindered, Spirit-filled prayer life. We cannot pray effectively without the leadership of the Holy Spirit. Paul tells us, in Romans 8:26-27, that it is the Spirit who makes intercession for us, and who helps our infirmities. We do not know what we should pray for, but the Spirit shows us.

"Likewise the Spirit also helpeth our infirmities: for we know not what we should pray for as we ought: but the Spirit itself maketh intercession for us with groanings which cannot be uttered. And he that searcheth the hearts knoweth what is the mind of the Spirit, because he maketh intercession for the saints according to the will of God."

Seventeen times in the four gospels, Jesus instructs us to pray. Notice that in Matthew 5:44, the very first time He tells us to pray, He tells us to pray for those who despitefully use and persecute us! Why do you think He put such great emphasis on praying for those people who do cruel things to us? Jesus knew that He would be cursed, mocked, used and persecuted while He was on this earth. He knew that this would be done by His own people, but that, because of who He was, He also knew that His love for them was so great He would love them unconditionally. He knew that being able to pray for someone who had intentionally hurt us would reflect a godly quality in our Christian character, and it would also teach us to love even our enemies just as Jesus loved and gave His life for those who used and persecuted Him.

I think the greatest lesson Jesus wants us to learn from this, however, is that by praying for our enemies, we can truly see that there is power in prayer. Through a dedicated prayer life, we have an unlimited access to the love of the Father that Jesus is talking about in this specific scripture.

Our prayer life is our means of fellowship and communication with God. That is why we must set time aside every day to be alone with Him. We must take our prayer life very seriously. We can't expect answers, results, or quick relief from our burdens if we pray only at a convenient time for us.

Basically, summing it all up, without prayer we remain babes in Christ. We have no personal relationship with God. Without prayer, we have no fellowship, comfort, peace, or joy within us. Prayer is our number one resource and responsibility in our pursuit of becoming Christ-like.

2. Faith

Living by faith means trusting in something or someone that we can't see. Webster's defines faith as "an unquestioning belief." The apostle Paul gives us a beautiful definition of faith in Hebrew 11:1-3 when he says, "Now faith is the substance of things hoped for, the evidence of things not seen. For by it the elders obtained a good report. Through faith we understand that the worlds were framed by the word of God, so that things which are seen were not made of things which do appear."

Jesus says, in Acts 26:18, that we are sanctified by faith. In Acts 15:9, we learn that our hearts are purified by faith. We are saved by faith in Romans 10:9-10. In Acts 13:39, we see that we are justified by faith.

Our spiritual condition can only prosper and be revived through faith. We must choose to believe in what we can't see; we must choose to hope for the second coming of Jesus Christ. We must exercise our faith in God the Father, God the Son, and God the Holy Spirit.

The majority of Christians today are so burdened down with the pressures, trials, temptations, and tribulations of life that their faith in God has dwindled to little or none. It's all they can do to just pray to God, much less believe that they can receive from Him.

My point is that we must first experience our faith by asking for something until we receive it. We might then exercise our faith by asking one time and believing that what we ask for is on the way or that God's divine will is going to be done in the matter. The ability to experience and exercise our faith is based on the knowledge, love, and desire that we have in Jesus Christ.

The second thing we must do to exercise our faith is to walk by faith. Walking by faith is serving God and going forward with God even when we can't see or don't know what is ahead of us. Walking by faith produces righteousness.

Romans 4 gives us a clear principle of walking by faith, using Abraham as the perfect example. The whole purpose for walking by faith is to show God that no matter what He tells us to do, or where He may send us, we will go, resting on the promises of His Word. Romans 4:20-21 says, "He staggered not at the promise of God through unbelief; but was strong in faith, giving glory to God; [21] And being fully persuaded that, what he had promised, he was able also to perform."

When God wants you to do something, and you can't see where it's going to lead you, don't be afraid. Don't quit. Instead, go on and do what He's telling you to do, showing Him your willingness to serve Him by walking in faith. To know what is ahead of us is to walk by sight, but to be willing to venture out into the unknown for the sake of Jesus Christ is to wholly walk by faith.

I could go on forever telling you what faith can do for you, but I'll finish with this last thing. This is the most comforting assurance of all to me, and we find it in First John 5:4. It says, "For whatsoever is born of God overcometh the world: and this is the victory that overcometh the world, even our faith."

3. Study

Second Timothy 2:15 says, "Study to show thyself approved unto God, a workman that needeth not to be ashamed, rightly dividing the word of truth."

According to Strong's Exhaustive Concordance, the simple definition for study is "intensive intellectual effort." The word study is found only three times in the Bible (in Ecclesiastes 12:12, First Thessalonians 4:11, and Second Timothy 2:15). In order to be properly motivated, we need to know why it is so important for us to study God's Word, Who it is that teaches us to interpret the Bible, and how we can become better students of God's Word. In my personal studies, I have found that there are nine basic principles to go by in these matters. They are:

1. Pray before you study.
2. Have a willingness to want to know God's Word.
3. Get away to a quiet place.
4. Search the Scriptures until you find something that interests you.
5. Seek the truth.
6. Never get frustrated by what you don't understand.
7. Use tools such as a simple dictionary or a Bible concordance to teach you the definitions of Bible words. Remember, a workman must have tools.
8. Apply what the Holy Spirit teaches you to your own life.
9. Share what you learn with someone else.

4. Obedience

The final responsibility we are to uphold is obedience. We can pray, have faith in God, and study every day of our lives, but if we refuse to obey God, we are wasting our time. We can't have one without the other; prayer, faith, study, and obedience all go hand in hand.

Acts 5:29 tells us "We ought to obey God rather than man." Sometimes Satan hinders us in our obedience. Again, James 4:7 says, "Submit yourselves therefore to God. Resist the devil, and he will flee from you."

To obey is to be submissive to the will of God. We so often choose man's will over God's, forcing Him to deal with us in an unpleasant way just to show us our disobedience. If we become obedient to God, we allow our salvation to be shown; we also allow God room for His will and good pleasure to be experienced in our lives.

Philippians 2:12-13 says, "Wherefore, my beloved, as ye have always obeyed, not as in my presence only, but now much more in my absence, work out your own salvation with fear and trembling. For it is God which worketh in you both to will and to do of his good pleasure." God's rewards for our obedience are beyond our comprehension.

What are our purposes and intentions, and how far are we willing to go to please our Heavenly Father? Keep in mind while studying this that you must be born-again to be in obedience to the Father, and remember that obedience is what produces righteousness unto God.

Obedience is also a willingness to serve God. To be obedient means to sacrifice what you want to do for what God wants you to do. If we can discipline ourselves to serve God all during the week rather than just on Sundays, imagine how much greater our blessings would be and how much more obedient we would become. I beg you to put your trust in Him, not looking back at what you were, but looking ahead to what you can become through Jesus Christ. The victory is yours in all things through Him.

Always remember that no matter how much you learn about God, or how much you grow in Him, or how much you suffer for His sake, there is always more to learn and more room to grow. Still, we must never stop spreading what we know. Reach forth for the things that are before; watch and wait! Be ready and prepared for the coming of the Lord.

If we are going to survive this present day we must get busy in making over our spiritual relationship with God. Makeovers are painful but the Bible teaches us this in Hebrews 12:11-13, "Now no chastening for the present seemeth to be joyous, but grievous: nevertheless afterward it yieldeth the peaceable fruit of righteousness unto them which are exercised thereby. [12]Wherefore lift up the hands which hang down, and the feeble knees; [13]And make straight paths for your feet, lest that which is lame be turned out of the way; but let it rather be healed."

As we face the present circumstances of our lives, healing will take place in different time frames. God's time frame is not always ours. Our response to present day problems often determines the speed of healing and/or deliverance.

How are you responding to your present battles?

- ☐ With fear
- ☐ With anger
- ☐ With doubt
- ☐ With faith
- ☐ With trust
- ☐ With hopelessness
- ☐ Your control
- ☐ God's control
- ☐ Through prayer
- ☐ In silence
- ☐ In rebellion
- ☐ Other

What do you want God to do in your present circumstances? _____

_____

Let's face our circumstances right now with God. He is waiting to speak to you. He has instructions for you that will extremely change your heart, give you hope, and renew you inside so that you deal with present situations in the Spirit rather than through the flesh. God understands that our hearts get shattered. He knows that our expectations have turned to disappointment. He understands when we feel betrayed and deceived by those closest to us. He is ever present in our present battles.

How do we survive when we feel defeated?

1. Cry out to God
2. Express your pain
3. Confess your feelings
4. Make God your counselor
5. Find the lesson in it

We must remember that God is the Great Physician. He is standing with you right now in your present warfare. He is protecting you while He is your strength. He wants to use this in your life to make you more like Him.

Daily Reflections: *Your Thoughts on Today's Study*

_____

_____

_____

_____

_____

_____

_____

_____

Prayer Journal: *Your Prayer on Today's Study*

_____

_____

_____

_____

_____

_____

_____

Day 4   *Preparing for the Future*

I Thessalonians 5:23-24: *"And the very God of peace sanctify you wholly; and I pray God your whole spirit and soul and body be preserved blameless unto the coming of our Lord Jesus Christ. [24]Faithful is he that calleth you, who also will do it."*

It is an amazing thing that we will dwell in our past, bring it into our present, and pattern daily living on the past and present. Isn't it strange that we would plan our future based on how the past has treated us and what is going on in our lives in the present?

Think about it: Most of us have decided that if Mom died with heart disease then we will, too. If Daddy battled depression, we will be victims of it also. And, I love this one: My whole family was large, so I'm going to be, too. So, we build our future on overeating, family curses, financial insecurities and physical ailments. Instead of determining to break these bondages, we settle ourselves to the fact that we are going to die early, poor and obese! We live in the mentality of "eat, drink and be merry, for tomorrow we die!"

WRONG ANSWER!

"God wants to bless our lives so that we always look forward to tomorrow."

Our Scripture text should break this mentality. There are two phrases in our text that teach us about preparing for the future. They are:

1. Sanctify Wholly: These words from the Holy Word are the reason we must prepare for the future. This phrase teaches us that God will purify (sanctify) us wholly (complete to the end; absolutely perfect). We should purpose in our hearts to live in His peace, protection and presence for this reason. Because God is making us completely pure, we have no reason to give up on a prosperous, joyful future. God wants to bless our lives so that we always look forward to tomorrow.

   Yesterday is past; yesterday is gone.
   Today is present, and it is fading.
   Tomorrow is the future, and tomorrow is ahead.

While God is wholly sanctifying us, His desire is that we:

A. Make Plans for the Future. He wants our future to be set on things above, not on the things of this earth. We should plan our future accordingly.
B. Set Goals for Ourselves. Learn more of His Word. Strive to become more spiritually minded and less worldly. Focus more attention on others than on self. Work on building a deeper relationship with God. Become a greater witness for Him.
C. Be Determined. Be determined to live for God, to identify and change your bad habits, and to overcome family and generational curses.

2. Preserved Blameless: Our Scripture text says, "I pray God your whole spirit and soul and body be preserved blameless." Preserved means guarded from loss or injury. Blameless means not arrested, unrebukeable.

We can prepare for a prosperous future because God has guarded us from Satan's tactics. As the body of believers, we should strive to live in and for Him. We can be assured that we are not only "present" material for His Kingdom work, but He is preparing our lives for future Kingdom work. We must put on the whole armor of God daily in order to be preserved blameless. Ephesians 6:14-18 lists this armor ("Stand therefore, having your loins girt about with truth, and having on the breastplate of righteousness; [15]And your feet shod with the preparation of the gospel of peace; [16]Above all, taking the shield of faith, wherewith ye shall be able to quench all the fiery darts of the wicked. [17]And take the helmet of salvation, and the sword of the Spirit, which is the word of God: [18]Praying always with all prayer and supplication in the Spirit, and watching thereunto with all perseverance and supplication for all saints."):

1. Have your loins girt about with truth (v. 14).
2. Having on the breastplate of righteousness (v. 14).
3. Your feet shod with the preparation of the gospel of peace (v. 15).
4. Taking the shield of faith (v. 16).
5. The helmet of salvation (v. 17).
6. The sword of the spirit (v. 17).
7. Praying always (v. 18).

If we could ever acclimate to suiting up with God's protective and powerful armor daily, then we would be totally prepared for whatever the future delivers. This armor completes the extreme makeover that will carry us boldly into the future.

God's protective armor will:

1. Deliver us from the family curse.
2. Restore our righteousness.
3. Allow us to face the future with peace.

4. Secure us a future with God in Heaven.
5. Guide us into truth.
6. Equip us to fight our adversaries.
7. Build our faith for what's ahead.

Our future in Christ is bright. Jesus said He would never leave or forsake us. He is going into the future with us, regardless of what lies ahead. And the joy of it all is that He already knows what it is that lies ahead. The assurance of this allows us to have peace about the future. Ephesians 6:10 says, "Finally, my brethren, be strong in the Lord."

We don't know what tomorrow, next week, next month or next year holds, but with the Lord, we can face it with joy and excitement. God knows our future so well that He has something to say about it today. His voice will challenge you to charge ahead, to move forward in your relationship with Him, and to carry on in your service for Him.

If we could plan out the days ahead according to our will, there would be no need to depend on God. Our lives would be exactly what we wanted them to be. Our lives would be settled and our future would be secure. We would set ourselves up right! We would never want for anything. Our marriages would be perfect, and our banks accounts would be forever increasing. Our children would have everything they wanted and then some. Our homes would be the finest on the block, and they'd be paid in full! Are you getting the picture? Have you noticed that everything I've mentioned here is all about "US"?

If we controlled the future, we would set ourselves up as gods, and we would leave the one true God out of our lives. We would set ourselves up for present security that would eventually lead to future failure, because we know that without God we can do nothing! The good news is that we can prepare for a brighter and blessed future regardless of our present circumstances.

What preparations are you making for the future? _____
_____

Do they involve God? _____
_____

Will they be of eternal value? _____
_____

When do you plan to start? The future starts in the very next second. _____
_____

The precepts for a confident future are:

1. Salvation – The presence and power of God
2. Sacrifice – Giving up one thing for the sake of another

3. Separation – Set apart from things of the world
4. Steadfastness – firm, persistent and determined
5. Satisfaction – completely fulfilled
6. Shield – a protective armor
7. Silence – a time to listen

God has great plans for your future. You do not have to approach tomorrow in fear and doubt. God will instruct and guide you into all truth.

What's coming up in your future that you need God's voice and instruction in? There is no need to fear. God will be right there with you. He knows the day, the time, the place and the circumstances. Instead of living in fear, we should be getting excited about what He is going to do. God has the answer, the understanding and the solution.

Record your greatest fear about the future in the space below: _____
_____

Your main concern about the future should be where you will be spiritually. God knows what the circumstances are doing to you, and He wants to speak to you about them. He wants to move you into the future with great faith and determination in Him.

Daily Reflections: Your Thoughts on Today's Study

_____

_____

_____

_____

_____

_____

_____

Prayer Journal: *Your Prayer on Today's Study*

_____

_____

_____

_____

_____

_____

_____

Day 5   *The Finished Work*

John 19:30: *"When Jesus therefore had received the vinegar, he said, It is finished: and he bowed his head, and gave up the ghost."*

Jesus gave Himself in a cruel, agonizing death; yet, He wouldn't have had it any other way. The Son of God chose to take our place at Calvary so that we could live victoriously-free from death, hell, and the grave! From that day forward, there would be no need for a high priest to offer a sacrifice for the sins of the people. There would be no need for the shedding of blood. Christ's blood was the final token of sacrifice for sin. Prophecies had been fulfilled; covenants, promises, and dispensations were recorded in history as the dispensation of grace unfolded on Golgotha's Hill. Thirty-three and a half years before this day, the promise of a Messiah had been fulfilled. Now the blood covenant of the Old Testament was final and complete through the death, burial and resurrection of our Lord and Savior Jesus Christ. The extreme makeover had taken place, and it was successful.

"A final sacrifice for sin has been given; there will never be a need for another."

God can again look upon His people as they receive Jesus as their Savior. By His grace through faith we are given the free gift of salvation. We no longer have to worry about losing our salvation or being rejected. When Jesus died for our sins, it was final. In the ninth hour, Jesus bowed His head and died. In Scripture, nine is the number of finality or completion. Yes, a final sacrifice for sin has been given; there will never be a need for another. The sacrifice was the ultimate, perfect, spotless One, and no other man could have done it. Jesus was the only One fit for the journey. He loved us enough to give His life so that we could have life more abundantly.

As Jesus faced His journey, He knew what the future held for Him. Like any human, He dreaded its pain, its rejection, and its stress, but being destitute of His Father's love would have been the greatest agony of all. He knew that with the world's sin on Himself, His Father could not look upon Him, yet His love for us compelled Him to become the final sacrifice. Why?

He knew that His death would produce eternal life for all who would believe! Romans 8:1-2 says, "There is therefore now no condemnation to them which are in Christ Jesus, who walk not after the flesh, but after the Spirit. For the law of the Spirit of life in Christ Jesus hath made me free from the law of sin and death."

Jesus died in our place, and through His death we are justified. He made us worthy of life by being sin's sacrifice. First Peter 3:18 says, "For Christ also hath once suffered for sins, the just for the unjust, that he might bring us to God, being put to death in the flesh, but quickened by the Spirit."

For Jesus Christ, once is all it took. He will never have to hang upon the cross again for our sins. He died for them once and for all the first time. First John 1:7 says, "But if we walk in the light, as he is in the light, we have fellowship one with another, and the blood of Jesus Christ his Son cleanseth us from all sin."

The blood cleanses us from all sin. Jesus died for every sin - yesterday's, today's, and tomorrow's. Why would we think that we are not forgiven? The truth is spread out before us in plain sight. He was such a perfect sacrifice that one time finished it all. This is proven again for us in Hebrews 7:26-27, which says, "For such an high priest became us, who is holy, harmless, undefiled, separated from sinners, and made higher than the heavens; Who needeth not daily, as those high priests, to offer up sacrifice, first for his own sins, and then for the people's: for this he did once, when he offered up himself."

The word "once" is as final in the original Greek tense as Christ's sacrifice was. It is found in Hebrews 9:11-12, which says, "But Christ being come an high priest of good things to come, by a greater and more perfect tabernacle, not made with hands, that is to say, not of this building; Neither by the blood of goats and calves, but by his own blood he entered in once into the holy place, having obtained eternal redemption for us." Nowhere in the Bible is it recorded that Christ's crucifixion was a temporary sacrifice for sin. The Word of God is completely contrary to this. Everywhere in Scripture we find proof that Christ died for sin once and for all. He is the eternal sacrifice! He is eternal life!

The penalty for sin was paid at Calvary. Now we can go straight to God if we have received Jesus as our Savior. We don't have to live every day of our lives wondering if our sins are going to send us to hell. They are not! Jesus has already died for them. The only thing that's going to send you to hell is not receiving Jesus Christ into your heart as your Lord and Savior.

If you are saved, you have been made free from the chains of Satan, the world, and the flesh. You can't be saved today and lost tomorrow. If you have realized you are a sinner, confessed your sin to God, repented of your sins, asked Christ to save you, and received and believed Him by faith, then you are being sanctified (set apart and made holy) day by day through the grace of God. You are being made complete in Christ Jesus. He is putting the finishing touches on your life. He is making you more pleasing to Himself.

My friend, let's not fret over our position in Christ Jesus. Let's humble ourselves before Him and ask Him to confirm within us what our true position is. We can never grow in grace if we are always worried about dying and going to hell. Jesus did not die for your sins for you to live with the fear of losing your salvation. He died to bring you life, peace, and joy - and that more abundantly!

He died for you to be:

Fashioned
In Him, a
New
Image.
Sanctified
Heirs-
Eternally
Delivered!

Oh, what a Savior!

Daily Reflections: Your Thoughts on Today's Study

_____

_____

_____

_____

_____

_____

_____

Prayer Journal: Your Prayer on Today's Study

_____

_____

_____

_____

_____

_____

_____

Chapter 2

Facing the Facts

Ephesians 6:12: *"For we wrestle not against flesh and blood, but against principalities, against powers, against the rulers of the darkness of this world, against spiritual wickedness in high places."*

Each morning most of us wake up and tell ourselves it's going to be a beautiful morning, but deep inside we feel like it's just a lie. In our hearts and minds, we pray for "this day" to be trouble and worry free. Others are born with a more positive outlook and can find good in any bad situation, but those who tend to see only the negative lose control at the first hint of a problem.

Regardless of your outlook, the fact of the matter is that we live in a tainted world, and its prince is Satan himself. He tries to make each of us feel gloom, despair, and hopelessness. He loves and thrives off of your weaknesses of the flesh. He simply uses them to keep you downtrodden and defeated.

Hopelessness, gloom and despair are the lies and deceptions of Satan. The truth is, our battle is not with ourselves or with God. Our battle is with the rulers of darkness. We are plagued daily by the father of lies, the thief of peace, and the murderer of joy. He loves to remind us of our past, our failures and our sin. We find ourselves wounded and feeling unworthy to overcome life's obstacles.

"God wants us to be positive and faithful. He is not our enemy."

In the end, we end up depressed, stressed, unmotivated and totally exhausted in this race called life. The principality, the power, and the ruler of darkness of this world has done a makeover on us, and it's not a pretty sight.

In spite of how the facts stack up against us, we have hope, because there is a higher power than this ruler of darkness. This higher power is God almighty, and we need to recognize and understand Him as the Father of truth.

Satan is the father of lies and the ruler of darkness. God is the Father of truth and the light of this world. God longs to pour His light into the darkness of Satan that tries to cover our lives. God wants us to be positive and faithful. He is not our enemy. God does not remind us of our past and failures. He loves us in spite of all of these things.

God wants to do another makeover in the life of "whosoever will." He wants to remove the past, the pain and the problems. Let's face the facts about ourselves today, carry the facts to God, and allow Him to renovate our lives.

1. List below the facts of your life:

_____

_____

2. What is in your past that still affects your life, your self-esteem, and, most of all, your relationship with God? _____

_____

3. How do these things affect your life? Has it left you angry, bitter, rebellious, confused, etc...? _____

_____

4. What pain are you carrying today? _____

_____

5. What problems do you need to confess to God today? _____

_____

For the next five days, we will allow God to renovate our hearts and minds as we deal with the issues of life that cause us to need reconstructive surgery from the inside out.

Day 1   *Who*

Psalm 55:12-14: *"For it was not an enemy that reproached me; then I could have borne it: neither was it he that hated me that did magnify himself against me; then I would have hid myself from him: But it was thou, a man mine equal, my guide, and mine acquaintance. We took sweet counsel together, and walked unto the house of God in company."*

Wow! David boldly states in our Scripture text that his persecution, pain and problems were coming from someone closest to him, someone he knew, loved and even went to church with. David said they took sweet counsel together. His heart was shattered that this person had come against him and sought to do him harm.

Who was this person? What did he do for David to wish death upon him (v. 15)? Maybe it was someone who wanted David's position. Maybe it was someone who was jealous, competitive, and determined to destroy David just to get what they wanted out of life. Perhaps this person was hurting on the inside, and they wanted David to hurt, too. Maybe he was just crying out for help. Regardless of whether it was friend or foe, David handled it God's way.

1. He did not treat them as he had been treated. He simply prayed for them. v. 16
2. He prayed for protection for himself. v. 17
3. He rested in peace. v. 18
4. He realized the facts about this person when he said in v. 21, "The words of his mouth were smoother than butter, but war was in his heart: his words were softer than oil, yet were they drawn swords."
5. David knew who he could trust and who would sustain him. v. 22-23

Who is the "who" in your life causing you grief? _____
_____

How are you handling the facts?_____
_____

We can be assured that the "who" in this chapter of David's life fit the role of principalities and powers, rulers of darkness and spiritual wickedness in high places. David was a man with authority under God's authority. Thus, many wanted David and righteousness destroyed. The same holds true for your life.

Daily Reflections: Your Thoughts on Today's Study

_____

_____

_____

_____

_____

_____

_____

Prayer Journal: Your Prayer on Today's Study

_____

_____

_____

_____

_____

_____

_____

Day 2   *What*

Psalm 55:22: *"Cast thy burden upon the LORD, and he shall sustain thee: he shall never suffer the righteous to be moved."*

Yesterday, we faced the facts that we have enemies, and our enemies are not necessarily strangers. Usually, our enemies are those closest to us, those we trust and confide in. They are the people we live with, serve with and work with. Perhaps these people are not true enemies, but they are the people that Satan, the father of lies, uses to cause us to get angry and rebellious with God.

David didn't tell us in Psalm 55 what his battle was, but we do know that it did not cause him to get angry and rebellious with God. Instead, he cast his burden upon the Lord. Regardless of what your battle may be, God is the sustainer, not the destroyer. That means that He will keep you through this battle.

Although David didn't mention his specific battle, he did tell us that it was evil, wicked and that death was deserved. It also brought him great sorrow. Psalm 55:4-8 show us how this battle affected David inside:

My heart is sore pained within me: and the terrors of death are fallen upon me. Fearfulness and trembling are come upon me, and horror hath overwhelmed me. And I said, Oh that I had wings like a dove! for then would I fly away, and be at rest. Lo, then would I wander far off, and remain in the wilderness. Selah I would hasten my escape from the windy storm and tempest.

Is this the kind of pain that your "what" is causing in your life? David's feelings are listed below. Underline each one that relates to you:

      Heart is severely pained
      Terror of death
      Fear and trembling are upon you
      Horror overwhelms you
      Wanting to run and hide

I don't know the "what" in your life, but the Lord surely does. He knows how you have responded to it, and He knows how it has affected your life as a born again believer. He knows your "what" even if your not a born again believer. Whether you are a believer or a non-believer, God can and will deliver you.

The child of God can cast their burden upon the Lord and he will sustain you. He will never allow the righteous to be moved. The unbeliever can cry out for salvation, and the Lord will hear and save. Then he, too, can be sustained and delivered.

Yesterday, you identified the "who" in your life. Can you identify the "what" today? _____

_____

How has this thing affected your life as a Christian? _____
_____
_____

Have you used it as an excuse to not serve the Lord? _____

You can't change the "what" in your life, but you can change how you respond!

Daily Reflections: Your Thoughts on Today's Study

_____

_____

_____

_____

_____

_____

_____

_____

_____

Prayer Journal: *Your Prayer on Today's Study*

_____

_____

_____

_____

_____

_____

_____

Day 3 *When*

Psalm 55:23: *"But thou, O God, shalt bring them down into the pit of destruction: bloody and deceitful men shall not live out half their days; but I will trust in thee."*

When did all of the events described in Psalm 55 happen to David? Based on the first few verses, it had to be in his time of service to the Lord. David was a man after God's own heart. Paul stated in 2 Timothy 2:12, we must suffer for Christ if we will reign with Him.

The painful problems of our lives may have happened when we were children or just before we reached our goals in life. They may have happened when we thought life was at its best. It doesn't matter when they happened. The thing that matters is when you gave it to the Lord. When you trust Him with your conflict, victory will be present.

"When you trust Him with your conflict, victory will be present."

God is so all-knowing in our lives that He knows the date, place, time and purposes of your "when." The "when" for most people seems to be at a time when they were already oppressed and hopeless. As the saying goes, life seems to kick us when we're already down. These are the tactics of the principalities, powers, rulers of darkness and spiritual wickedness in high places. The enemy strikes most effectively when we are weak and vulnerable.

On the flip side of this tactic, the enemy also strikes when we feel that nothing can stop us. The enemy will hit us in the time when we see God working and feel that He has a hedge of protection around us. The enemy sneaks in when we're on a spiritual high, and he seeks to defile us.

Satan throws wrenches into our lives whenever and wherever he sees the opportunity. "But thou, O God, shalt bring them down into the pit of destruction: bloody and deceitful men shall not live out half their days; but I will trust in thee (Psalm 55:23)." When we trust in God, the "when" no longer matters. The promise that He will bring our enemies to destruction becomes our victory.

How long has it been since your last battle? _____

_____

When did you turn it over to God? _____

_____

What was your spiritual state when this battle came upon you? Circle your answer below:

Confident   Oppressed   Excited   Defeated   Weak   Hopeless

Daily Reflections: Your Thoughts on Today's Study

_____

_____

_____

_____

_____

_____

_____

Prayer Journal: Your Prayer on Today's Study

_____

_____

_____

_____

_____

_____

_____

Day 4   *Where*

Psalm 55:10-11: *"Day and night they go about it upon the walls thereof: mischief also and sorrow are in the midst of it. Wickedness is in the midst thereof: deceit and guile depart not from her streets."*

Where the wounds in our lives were inflicted is a great factor in why we do or do not serve the Lord with liberty and confidence. The place of battle always brings memories of pain and devastation. The evil forces that come against us will seek to remind us of the time and place of our conflict. In spite of the fact we have survived it (or else we wouldn't be reading this book today), the "where" factor can still control our growth as Christians.

So many people are still living in the "where" of their battles. If the battle was in church, they use that as an excuse not to go back to that church (or any other church for that matter). If the battle was at Mom's house, then they refuse to go back to Mom's. If the battle was at work, they just quit their job. Friends, we cannot continue to run from the places of our pain and confrontation. Conflict will find us wherever we go. Today's Scripture text reminds us that wickedness is in our midst. Deceit and guile dwell in our streets.

"We cannot continue to run from the places of pain and confrontation."

When I went away to write this book, I went under the leadership of the Lord. He called me away to a place of fasting and prayer, a place with no interruption or hindrances outside of my normal environment. I went where I felt God was leading me, but still, there was wickedness, deceit and guile were in the midst. The couple in the room next to mine continuously yelled and cursed at one another. We shared a balcony, and the wiles of Satan didn't stop until I went out onto the balcony with Bible in hand and sat next to them with beers in hand. They finally retreated to their room, and the attacks of the enemy on my solitude with God ended. Now I am praying for the opportunity to witness to this couple. My point is this: wherever you go, you will run into conflict and attack. You will have disturbances and distractions, but you don't have to run. You can stand in that place, with the Sword of the Spirit in hand, and fight the battle. The Word of God always prevails, every time in every place.

Go back to those places where the pain was inflicted and acknowledge the who, what, when and where. James 4:7 says, "Submit yourselves therefore to God. Resist the devil, and he will flee from you (James 4:7)."

Where are you in your relationship with God?_____

Where do you need to go to acknowledge your pain, conflict and wickedness?

_____

_____

Day and night you will journey through places of wickedness, mischief, deceit and guile. Submit yourself to God and He will protect you wherever you are.

Daily Reflections: Your Thoughts on Today's Study

_____

_____

_____

_____

_____

_____

_____

_____

_____

Prayer Journal: Your Prayer on Today's Study

_____

_____

_____

_____

_____

_____

_____

_____

Day 5 *Why*

Psalm 55:3: *"Because of the voice of the enemy, because of the oppression of the wicked: for they cast iniquity upon me, and in wrath they hate me."*

Why do bad things happen to good people? Why do little babies have to die? Why do Christians seem to suffer above the wicked? Why do innocent people become victims? All of these questions are legitimate, but they are easily answered with understanding. When bad things happen to us or to those we love, the first thing we do is to question God. "Lord, why did you let this happen? What kind of God are you?"

The ruler of darkness of this world has lied to us once again. In the midst of our pain, he shifts the blame to God. If we do not buy into the lie that God is directly to blame, Satan still plants the seed that if God didn't do it, He still allowed it to happen. After all, God has all power and dominion over the events in this world. This is exactly what the enemy wants you to think. Through the weakness of our minds, he causes us to be angry with and misunderstanding of God.

We must not forget the complete teachings of the Bible. Even though God is still on the throne, Satan is the prince of the power of this world. He roars about as a lion seeking whom he may devour. Bad things happen for many reasons:

- Because of the voice of the enemy.
- Because of the oppression of the wicked.
- Because of the iniquity upon us.
- Because we are hated for Christ's sake.

Colossians 1:16 says, "For by him were all things created, that are in heaven, and that are in earth, visible and invisible, whether they be thrones, or dominions, or principalities, or powers: all things were created by him, and for him." These things are allowed to happen in our lives so that we can:
Learn to hear God's voice over the voice of the enemy.

- See goodness over wickedness.
- Impute righteousness over iniquity.
- Apply love where hate abounds.

We will never understand why some things happen. We can, however, rest assured that we know all things happened for good to those who love the Lord and are called according to His purpose (Romans 8:28).

Can you find the good in your "why"? _____

Is Satan trying to shift blame to God? _____

What are you doing to renovate your mind on the matter?_____
_____

Daily Reflections: Your Thoughts on Today's Study

_____

_____

_____

_____

_____

_____

_____

_____

_____

Prayer Journal: Your Prayer on Today's Study

_____

_____

_____

_____

_____

_____

_____

Chapter 3

Dealing with Reality

John 16:32-33: *"Behold, the hour cometh, yea, is now come, that ye shall be scattered, every man to his own, and shall leave me alone: and yet I am not alone, because the Father is with me. ^{33}These things I have spoken unto you, that in me ye might have peace. In the world ye shall have tribulation: but be of good cheer; I have overcome the world."*

Jesus gave these words of comfort just before His death on Calvary. He left the disciples with the reality that they would get so caught up in the world and its temptations that they would forget about serving Him. This is why He said in verse 32: "Ye shall be scattered, every man to his own, and shall leave me alone: and yet I am not alone, because the Father is with me." We must understand that Jesus was talking to His disciples, the ones whom He loved and who loved Him. These disciples had witnessed His power and walked in His love.

"These things I have spoken unto you, that in me ye might have peace."

Jesus knew how they would respond when He was no longer with them in His fleshly body. The reality was that they would not remember all that He had taught them. He knew they would become victims of the world and its tribulations. He knew that they would become so weak in their own pain and grief that they would abandon all He had ever taught them. He knew they would give in to their:

- Flesh
- Failures
- Fatigue
- Faults
- Fears

Jesus tried to prepare them for such reality: "These things I have spoken unto you, that in me ye might have peace. In the world ye shall have tribulation: but be of good cheer; I have overcome the world."

The greatest reality of all is the fact that whatever comes into your life first had to go through God the Father, Jesus the Son and the Holy Spirit before it could get to you. Your life is hid with God in Christ Jesus. He is your hiding place, and nothing can get to you without God's permission. God puts a protective hedge around His own.

Day 1   The Flesh

John 16:33: *"These things I have spoken unto you, that in me ye might have peace. In the world ye shall have tribulation: but be of good cheer; I have overcome the world."*

In the world, we will have tribulation. Our flesh functions, feeds and falters in the world. We live under the pressures of what everyone else is, has or does. We thrive off of keeping up with those around us. We are deceived into thinking that we must build an image that will:

- Impress those around us.
- Gain social stature.
- Promote a prominent reputation

The reality is that we have become the victims of the fleshly ideals of others. We seek the applause of others over the approval of God.

Jesus tried to warn us of the tribulations of this world. He knew we would lose the peace and joy of who we are in Him because of the weaknesses of our flesh. Page after page in the Bible shows us that the flesh lusts against the Spirit. Paul warned us that the flesh is tainted with sin. David reminded us that we were created in sin. However, Romans 13:14 says, "But put ye on the Lord Jesus Christ, and make not provision for the flesh, to fulfil the lusts thereof."

"Jesus tried to warn us of the tribulations of this world."

Instead of wrestling with our flesh, we just give in to it. We give in to lust for food, finances, fame and folly. We never even consider the repercussions of our decisions.

The flesh is constantly at war with the Spirit. We want to blame our actions on Satan, but it is actually our self-will that determines whether we will be led by the flesh or by the Spirit. The power to overcome your flesh is found within if the Spirit abides there. When you were born again, the Spirit of God made you new on the inside. Now, you must allow Him to make you over on the outside as well.

In this world, you shall have tribulation, but be of good cheer. Jesus has overcome the world. Precious ones, remember these things:

1. You do not have to give in to your flesh.
2. You do not have to impress others.
3. You need only the approval of God.

What is the battle of your flesh? _____
_____

Are you blaming the devil, saying, "The devil made me do it"?_____
_____

Did Eve twist Adam's arm to make him eat the forbidden fruit? _____
_____

Just like Eve, you too will experience and battle:

- The lust of the flesh
- The lust of the eyes
- The pride of life.

All of these are connected with your flesh.

Daily Reflections: *Your Thoughts on Today's Study*

_____

_____

_____

_____

_____

_____

_____

_____

Prayer Journal: *Your Prayer on Today's Study*

_____

_____

_____

_____

_____

_____

_____

Day 2   *Failures*

Matthew 26:74-75: *"Then began he to curse and to swear, saying, I know not the man. And immediately the cock crew.* [75]*And Peter remembered the word of Jesus, which said unto him, Before the cock crow, thou shalt deny me thrice. And he went out, and wept bitterly."*

Talk about feeling like a failure! You can be sure that Peter felt just that. Jesus had forewarned Peter about his denial, but in his heart, Peter believed that he would stand with Jesus no matter the cost.

I love this story. The reality behind it is so fascinating. Peter did not fail Jesus. Peter failed Peter. Failure is when someone doesn't accomplish what is expected of them. It may be their expectations or the expectations of others that they fail to meet. Nevertheless, you cannot fail someone who knows you better than you know yourself.

Jesus knew Peter's heart, but He also knew Peter's weaknesses. This is why Jesus warned Peter of the failure to come. Jesus was simply revealing to Peter, "Hey, I know you better than you know yourself." "Peter remembered the word of Jesus, which said unto him, Before the cock crow, thou shalt deny me thrice. And he went out, and wept bitterly."

"You cannot fail someone who knows you better than you know yourself."

With bitter tears of disappointment, Peter felt ashamed and guilty. I can almost hear him thinking: "Jesus told me I would do this." Then, "I really thought in my heart that I would stand with Him." Feeling like a failure, he walks away defeated and ashamed.

This is exactly how the enemy wanted him to respond. Satan didn't want Peter to rise above his failure. He didn't want Peter to feel loved by God. He didn't want Peter to proclaim the promises that Jesus taught before He was crucified. Satan wanted Peter to dwell in his failures.

The enemy wants you to do the same thing. Your life with God is no different than Peter's. He knows you better than you know yourself. Therefore, He has no expectations of you, and you can't let Him down. You have expectations of yourself; others have expectations of you. Jesus already knows what you are going to do. He knows when you will receive Him, reject Him, love Him and deny Him. He knows the choices you will make in life. He knows you from the inside out. Therefore, your feelings of failure are brought on by others, Satan and yourself.

Jesus is standing with open arms, waiting for you to bring your failures and lay them at His feet. He's waiting to renew your mind. He longs to release you from the bondage of failure. He released Peter, and He will release you. Mark 16:6-7 says, "And he saith unto them, Be not affrighted: Ye seek Jesus of Nazareth, which was crucified: he is risen; he is not here: behold the place where they laid him. [7]But go your way, tell his disciples and Peter that he goeth before you into Galilee: there shall ye see him, as he said unto you."

Did you catch what was stated in that Scripture? It said, "Tell his disciples and Peter." Jesus was alive! He was not angry with Peter, and He wanted Peter to know that. Failure does not destroy God's relationship with us. It destroys our relationship with Him because we allow it to do so.

Do not live in your failures. Do not allow others to remind you of your failures. Make your failures stepping stones, not stumbling blocks.

What failures are you reminded of daily?_____
_____

Who brings these failures to your remembrance?_____
_____

Have you confessed these feelings of failure to God? _____
_____

Do you feel like God is ashamed of you or that He does not love you because of your failures? _____
_____

What does Romans 8:35-39 say about this?_____
_____
_____

Daily Reflections: *Your Thoughts on Today's Study*

_____

_____

_____

_____

_____

_____

_____

_____

Prayer Journal: *Your Prayer on Today's Study*

_____

_____

_____

_____

_____

_____

_____

_____

Day 3   *Fatigue*

1 Peter 5:7: *"Casting all your care upon him; for he careth for you."*

The words of 1 Peter 5:7 imply throwing all of our anxiety and fatigue upon God. When Jesus said we would have tribulation in this world, the tribulation included fatigue. Fatigue means a disturbed state of mind produced by real or imaginary fears. Jesus knew that we could only survive the stresses of this life through dependence on Him.

As Christians, we should be totally dependent on God for all things. We overcome fatigue through discipline. If we fail to remember God's promises, study His Word and pray without ceasing, we will find ourselves so stressed that we turn to the things of this world for relief. Sinful things such as drugs, food, sex, money, pleasures, and unhealthy relationships, will become our stress relievers, but these temporary fixes only create more stress and fatigue.

Fatigue is not only a physical state; it also affects our mind and emotions. Its root cause is fear. Let's get this straight: fatigue is caused by the fear of what we know and see as well as what we don't know and can't see. A diagnosis of terminal illness is a stressful thing. It causes great fatigue when we see danger ahead and know that we can't do anything about it. It tears our heart out to see loved ones hurting or to see someone struggling with addictions.

"We overcome fatigue through discipline."

Jesus was fatigued as He prayed in the garden. His sweat became as great drops of blood. He agonized over His journey to Golgotha. His fatigue stemmed from what was known. Jesus knew the things He would have to suffer so that we could have fellowship with God. Did His fatigue stop Him from completing the task? No! Jesus cast all His cares upon His Father, and in three days He arose victorious.

Jesus did not suffer fatigue from the things He did not know or could not see. He was God incarnate. He knew everything: past, present and future. Jesus can see all the way into eternity, and He has never feared the future. We don't have to fear the future, either, because we can cast our cares upon Him.

God cares about our stress. He sees just how fatigued we are. He knows that these things can make us physically, spiritually and mentally sick. God knows that most of our fatigue derives from the unknown, the unfixable and fear of the outcome.

Fatigue also stems from this world's demands. The fear of failure, shattered expectations, broken dreams, broken lives and sinful behaviors all lead to fatigue. The list of causes could go on and on. Some of the causes are real;

some are imaginary. The only way to be released from them all is to cast them upon Jesus, knowing that He cares for us.

Jesus will bear your burdens for you. He will protect you in your times of stress, and He will lift you up above the shadows. Jesus is looking upon you right now. He sees the effects that fatigue has brought upon you.

Fatigue changes several things about us:

- Our countenance drops
- Our behavior changes
- Our moods become unbalanced
- Our health suffers
- Our spirits struggle
- Oppression hovers over us
- Depression smothers us

What is causing fatigue in your life? _____

_____

Is the cause of your fatigue real, imaginary or a combination of both? _____

_____

Separate the real causes from the imaginary:

Real: _____

_____

Imaginary: _____

_____

Fatigue can have many effects on us. Check the boxes below to indicate how it has affected you:

- ☐ Countenance
- ☐ Behavior
- ☐ Moods
- ☐ Health
- ☐ Spiritual
- ☐ Oppression
- ☐ Depression
- ☐ Other

Have you cast your cares upon the Lord? _____

_____

Daily Reflections: Your Thoughts on Today's Study

_____

_____

_____

_____

_____

_____

_____

_____

_____

Prayer Journal: Your Prayer on Today's Study

_____

_____

_____

_____

_____

_____

_____

_____

Day 4 *Fears*

2 Timothy 1:7: *"For God hath not given us the spirit of fear; but of power, and of love, and of a sound mind."*

Yesterday our study was on fatigue and the real and imaginary fears that cause it. Today, let's look at the reality of the things which cause fear in our lives. We will identify the author of fear and then remedy the problem.

Most of our fears stem from the old enemy, Satan. He may be the prince of the power of the air, but in reality he is running scared. He knows his final destination is an eternal lake of fire. Regardless of the powers that he flaunts in this world, the bottom line is that he is a defeated foe.

The kind of fears that we will address today do not come from God. They are weapons of the enemy to keep you terrified and cowered down in your relationship with God. I have listed some of these fears below. Can you relate to any of them?

- ☐ Failure
- ☐ Rejection
- ☐ The past
- ☐ The future
- ☐ The known
- ☐ The unknown
- ☐ Physical things
- ☐ Addictions
- ☐ Acceptance
- ☐ Approval

I've read somewhere that fear is anxiety caused by approaching danger. In this time and age, Satan seeks to change this definition. Satan wants fear to be defined as anxiety caused by anything in or approaching your life, whether it be danger or delight.

It's true. Fear has us so completely in its grip that we even fear delightful things. We fear even the blessings of God. Satan seeks to paralyze the body of Christ with a spirit of fear. His intentions are to keep us from living in a spirit of power, of love and of a sound mind. Fear's grip chokes these things out if we allow it to get a hold on us.

God is calling you to confront your fears. Cast them upon Him and live in His power. Allow God to rebuild what fear has torn down.

What is your greatest fear? _____

_____

How long have you carried this fear? _____

_____

Record Hebrews 13:6 below. Memorize this verse and repeat it to yourself when fear overtakes you. _____

_____

_____

Daily Reflections: Your Thoughts on Today's Study

_____

_____

_____

_____

_____

_____

_____

Prayer Journal: Your Prayer on Today's Study

_____

_____

_____

_____

_____

_____

_____

Day 5   *Faults*

Jude 24: *"Now unto him that is able to keep you from falling, and to present you faultless before the presence of his glory with exceeding joy."*

What is a fault? Simply defined, it is an imperfection. We all have some imperfections. In the eyes of man, there are levels or categories of faults. In the eyes of God, these imperfections are all sin, and He forgives them all.

Faults, imperfections and sin are all one and the same. First John 1:9 says, "If we confess our sins, he is faithful and just to forgive us *our* sins, and to cleanse us from all unrighteousness." Jesus, our Lord and Savior, can take our imperfections and use them to mature us through them.

The whole reason for Calvary was so that you could be presented spotless and blameless before God. Jesus bore your faults. You are released from them if you have received Christ as Lord of your life.

"The secret to overcoming faults is to confess them to God."

We often allow our faults to surface through our mind and our flesh. This is where sanctification becomes a two-fold process. You became sanctified (made holy) when you were saved. First Corinthians 3:16-17 says, "Know ye not that ye are the temple of God, and *that* the Spirit of God dwelleth in you? [17]If any man defile the temple of God, him shall God destroy; for the temple of God is holy, which *temple* ye are." When the Holy Spirit came to dwell in you, you were made new. Old things about your life, including your faults, were moved out so that holiness could move in. That was the instant work of sanctification in our lives.

Sanctification is also an ongoing, day by day process of renewing our minds. We must fight the faults of our flesh daily. The secret to overcoming faults is to confess them to God. When we turn to Him, He turns us from our sin. We have the power and presence of the Holy Spirit abiding within us. He makes intercession for you, even when you don't know how or what to pray.

The works of our flesh are the faults and imperfections that we battle daily. They are listed in Galatians 5:19-21. Can you find any of your faults listed in these verses? If so, list them here: _____

_____

What does Ephesians 4:22-24 teach us about the old man? _____

_____

Our Scripture text tells us that Jesus Christ is able to keep us from falling in spite of our faults. He will present you faultless before God. He will present you with exceeding joy. Remember, love covers a multitude of sin.

Daily Reflections: Your Thoughts on Today's Study

_____

_____

_____

_____

_____

_____

_____

_____

Prayer Journal: Your Prayer on Today's Study

_____

_____

_____

_____

_____

_____

_____

Chapter 4

Transforming the Mind

Romans 12:2: *"And be not conformed to this world: but be ye transformed by the renewing of your mind, that ye may prove what is that good, and acceptable, and perfect, will of God."*

Transformation takes place the moment Jesus becomes our Savior and takes up residence in our hearts. He makes our inside new. He takes that stony heart and makes it a heart of flesh. Jesus gives us a heart that feels, loves and overflows with compassion and forgiveness. On the inside, we literally become a new creation. The Bible says though our outward man perishes, the inward man is renewed day by day.

The outward man will perish. Even though we are renewed daily on the inside, we must also transform our minds daily. If we do not transform the mind, we will speed up the perishing process of the outward man. The mind is a fragile thing. It is the seat of Satan. He loves whispering sweet, subtle lies in your ear. He uses your mind for a battle ground, hoping to destroy God in you.

> ## "Transformation takes place the moment Jesus becomes our Savior and takes up residence in our hearts."

Let's look at how he transformed Eve's mind from innocence to conscience. He used lies to get Eve's attention. He questioned God's truths. He convinced her that if she ate of the tree of knowledge of good and evil that she would become this god-like superwoman.

The reason we have such great battles with our minds is that we have not transformed our thinking to God's truths. We conform more to the every day rituals of this world. Our minds are shaped by the following misguided thoughts:

- They do it; so can I.
- They get by with it; so can I.
- It's not hurting anyone.
- No one sees me doing it.
- Everyone does it; that makes it right.

Loved ones, this is the kind of thinking that brings chastisement upon your life. We must start transforming our minds right now by following these steps:

1. Confession
2. Correction
3. Conversion
4. Consecration
5. Commission

Day 1   *Confession*

1 John 1:9: *"If we confess our sins, he is faithful and just to forgive us our sins, and to cleanse us from all unrighteousness."*

Admitting who we are and what we're doing is confession. When our Scripture text tells us to confess our sins, it's instructing us to admit our ways. Admission to sin is the key to being forgiven and delivered.

Transformation takes place in our minds as we confess to God all of our sins. He is faithful and just to forgive us, cleanse us and turn us from our unrighteous ways.

In your mind, you will be told that your sin is too great. You will be told that you cannot be forgiven. You will even be told that you don't have to confess anything. These are lies and voices of the ruler of darkness.

Confession of sin is not the only thing we must admit to God. We must also confess our fears, problems, pains, temptations, insecurities and needs to Him. Confess your mind battles to Him. He is faithful to transform them if you will allow Him to do so.

I have learned that confession is a beautiful thing in my life. It draws me closer to God. It frees me from Satan's manipulation. As I confess things to God the things that are bothering me or controlling my mind, He is faithful to cleanse my mind. He always reminds me of a Bible verse, or He will send me a song to hum. Sometimes He just fills me with peace.

Please join me in the beauty of confession so that your mind can be transformed to righteousness.

What do you need to confess to God? _____

_____

What is going on in your mind that needs to be transformed to God's truths?__

_____

_____

What does James 4:7-8 have to say about this matter?_____

_____

_____

Daily Reflections: Your Thoughts on Today's Study

_____

_____

_____

_____

_____

_____

_____

_____

Prayer Journal: Your Prayer on Today's Study

_____

_____

_____

_____

_____

_____

_____

_____

Day 2   *Correction*

2 Timothy 3:16: *"All scripture is given by inspiration of God, and is profitable for doctrine, for reproof, for correction, for instruction in righteousness."*

Correction is a form of restoration. As we realize that things in our lives need to be corrected, God intervenes and helps us to restore our reputation as His children.

Dabbling in sin and listening to our minds instead of following our hearts will put us in a state of displeasure with God. The more we dabble, the more rebellious we become toward God.

The Bible says that a Father chastens those He loves. Chastening is often painful, but it will produce correction. The simple and pleasant form of correction for a believer is the Word of God. We are taught that it serves as a sword. It cuts to the dividing asunder of soul and spirit. The Word of God is a discerner of the thoughts and intents of the heart.

My friend, did you hear that? The Word of God is the correction rod for our lives. It discerns our thoughts (minds). It discerns the intentions of our hearts. If we want to be pleasing to God and free from the mind battles, then it is time we allow God's Word to correct our lives.

Confess your mistakes to God, starting with the most recent. _____

_____

God knows your heart better than you do. Ask Him to show you your true intentions as a Christian. Now, go to the Word and record His response here. _

_____

_____

Do you usually listen more to your mind or your heart? _____

_____

God calls each one of His children to correction. He prefers that we correct ourselves so that He doesn't have to correct us.

Daily Reflections: Your Thoughts on Today's Study

_____

_____

_____

_____

_____

_____

_____

Prayer Journal: Your Prayer on Today's Study

_____

_____

_____

_____

_____

_____

_____

Day 3   *Conversion*

Acts 3:19: *"Repent ye therefore, and be converted, that your sins may be blotted out, when the times of refreshing shall come from the presence of the Lord."*

Conversion is simply turning to God for abandonment of sin. As we turn to God, the following conversions take place. We are converted from:

- Darkness to light.
- Unrighteousness to righteousness.
- Evil to good.
- Hell to Heaven.
- Defeat to victory.
- Death to life.

The Scripture text tells us that conversion blots out our sins and times of refreshing come from none other than the Lord. Converting our lives into the holiness of God is the ultimate and eternal transformation. No other person is able to change us from death to life. No other person is able to completely and eternally blot out our sins.

"Conversion is simply turning to God for abandonment of sin."

Conversion is another two-fold principle. Conversion to God from sin is instant. However, conversion from the lust of the flesh, the temptations of the world and the deceptions of Satan are progressive as we turn to God from these strongholds.

Times of refreshing comes as we overcome our strongholds. Conversion is a product of our self-will. God will pour out His convictions upon us, but we must make the decision to heed to His call. Conversion is both salvation and the new life we have thereafter. Unless we convert our minds and change our ways, we will find ourselves in the ways of this world.

Do you know without a doubt that you have been converted? _____

What part of your life needs refreshing?_____
_____

Explain conversion's two-fold principle. _____
_____

List some of the strongholds you deal with in your life. _____

_____

Remember, times of refreshing come only from the presence of the Lord.

Daily Reflections: *Your Thoughts on Today's Study*

_____

_____

_____

_____

_____

_____

_____

_____

_____

Prayer Journal: *Your Prayer on Today's Study*

_____

_____

_____

_____

_____

_____

_____

Day 4   *Commission*

Matthew 28:18-20: *"And Jesus came and spake unto them, saying, All power is given unto me in heaven and in earth. [19]Go ye therefore, and teach all nations, baptizing them in the name of the Father, and of the Son, and of the Holy Ghost: [20]Teaching them to observe all things whatsoever I have commanded you: and, lo, I am with you alway, even unto the end of the world. Amen."*

Here, Jesus gives us the Great Commission. Every born again believer is commissioned to perform their duties and their service to the Lord.

The word commission means to be on a special assignment. When you were born again, your special assignment began. This special assignment or commission may not be what you would have chosen for yourself. God knew what His assignment for you would be, and He will equip you for the job.

We must abide by certain responsibilities while on this special assignment from the Lord. These responsibilities are found in every page of His blessed book. The Bible instructs us to:

- Share our faith.
- Teach righteousness.
- Win the lost.
- Preach the Gospel
- Love all mankind.
- Give to the poor.
- Help the hurting.

In our minds, we are already thinking of reasons why we can't do these things. Once again, wrong thinking patterns have led us to disobedience and insecurities. Between our own self-esteem and Satan's tactics, we have convinced ourselves that all these instructions are for someone else.

Precious children, we have a job to do, and God is expecting us to complete His work. He created us for His service. Our lives are not about what we want to do. Life is about magnifying Jesus Christ in a lost and dying world.

Do not allow your mind battles (such as fear, insecurities, doubt, timidity, low self-esteem, confusion, and lack of confidence) prevent you from attending to your special assignment.

It is evident that Jesus has the utmost confidence in you. If He didn't think you could or would do what He has called you to do, then He would not have called you for that service. John 15:16 says, "Ye have not chosen me, but I have chosen you, and ordained you, that ye should go and bring forth fruit, and *that* your fruit should remain: that whatsoever ye shall ask of the Father in my name, he may give it you."

When you are chosen by God, you are:

- Equipped.
- Qualified.
- Sanctified.

Take the challenge to put at least one of the following responsibilities into practice today:

1. Share your faith. Tell someone your salvation experience and why you love God.
2. Teach righteousness. Live or tell the difference of a holy life.
3. Win the lost. Share the plan of salvation.
4. Preach the Gospel. Preach simply means to share the Good News.
5. Love all mankind. Find someone unlovable and practice love on them.
6. Give to the poor. This is self-explanatory.
7. Help the hurting. Share words of encouragement, meet a financial need, lift someone in prayer, etc..

Once you have done at least one of these, you will realize that it was God working through you.

Daily Reflections: *Your Thoughts on Today's Study*

_____

_____

_____

_____

_____

_____

_____

_____

Prayer Journal: *Your Prayer on Today's Study*

_____

_____

_____

_____

_____

_____

_____

Day 5   *Consecration*

1 Peter 2:5: *"Ye also, as lively stones, are built up a spiritual house, an holy priesthood, to offer up spiritual sacrifices, acceptable to God by Jesus Christ."*

We learned yesterday that all of God's people are chosen and commissioned to be about the Father's business. Today we are appointed to total consecration. Consecration means to be devoutly dedicated to God's service.

Consecration is not a complicated process. You are sanctified (set apart) when you accept Christ as your Savior. The work Jesus did at Calvary justifies you (makes you acceptable to God). The position you hold as the bride of Christ consecrates you to God's service. Consecration appoints you to a life of purity and holiness.

Our Scripture text fully explains consecration. "As lively stones" refers to the fact that we were once dead in trespasses and sins but are now made alive unto God through the shed blood of Jesus Christ. We are to be built up as a spiritual house, meaning we should exemplify holiness in every area of our lives. Jesus Christ was the great and ultimate High Priest. He offered up His life as the final sacrifice for sin. Now, we are to be the holy priesthood and offer up spiritual sacrifices. This, my friends, is consecration.

"Consecration appoints you to a life of purity and holiness."

In simple terms, consecration can be explained from 1 Peter 1:15-16: "But as he which hath called you is holy, so be ye holy in all manner of conversation; [16]Because it is written, Be ye holy; for I am holy."

We have one additional requirement in this matter of consecration. The text said to offer up spiritual sacrifices. What does that mean?

The word spiritual means "relating to the human spirit or rational soul, as part of the man which is akin to God and serves as His instrument or organ."

The word sacrifice means "a sacrifice, victim." It also means the giving up of one thing for the sake of another.

Ephesians 5:2 describes spiritual sacrifices for us. "And walk in love, as Christ also hath loved us, and hath given himself for us an offering and a sacrifice to God for a sweetsmelling savour." Jesus gave His entire life to a cruel death as a spiritual sacrifice.

Mark 12:33 teaches us that spiritual sacrifices are above all other sacrifices. "And to love him with all the heart, and with all the understanding, and with all the soul, and with all the strength, and to love *his* neighbour as himself, is more than all whole burnt offerings and sacrifices."

The spiritual sacrifices listed here for us are: love with all the heart and understanding, with all the soul and strength and to love our neighbors as ourselves. Doing these things is more honorable than anything else we could offer or sacrifice.

Romans 12:1 gives us another definition of spiritual sacrifice: "I beseech you therefore, brethren, by the mercies of God, that ye present your bodies a living sacrifice, holy, acceptable unto God, *which is* your reasonable service."

From this point forward, we must heed to the fact that spiritual sacrifices require our complete self: body, heart, soul and mind consecrated to the service of the Lord. As we offer our lives as a spiritual sacrifice of worship, we are merely offering back to God what God has given to us in His only begotten Son: the ultimate sacrifice.

Hebrews 13:15-16 teaches us more about what spiritual sacrifices are: "By him therefore let us offer the sacrifice of praise to God continually, that is, the fruit of *our* lips giving thanks to his name. [16]But to do good and to communicate forget not: for with such sacrifices God is well pleased."

Spiritual sacrifices here are identified as:

- Continual praise to God.
- Our lips giving thanks.
- Doing good and communicating.

Hebrews 11:4 teaches that faith and righteousness are more excellent sacrifices. "By faith Abel offered unto God a more excellent sacrifice than Cain, by which he obtained witness that he was righteous, God testifying of his gifts: and by it he being dead yet speaketh."

Paul was certainly a consecrated, sacrificial man of God. In Philippians 2:17 he said, "Yea, and if I be offered upon the sacrifice and service of your faith, I joy, and rejoice with you all."

We can understand consecration as preparing ourselves in the holiness of God to present His Gospel through our lives. First Peter 2:9 seals the subject of consecration for us: "But ye *are* a chosen generation, a royal priesthood, an holy nation, a peculiar people; that ye should show forth the praises of him who hath called you out of darkness into his marvellous light."

Giving our lives over to the service of God will consecrate us as God's very own. We will neither act nor look the same. God's holiness changes our appearance, our behavior and our desires.

Have you consecrated yourself to God's service? _____

What part of your life do you need to offer up as a spiritual sacrifice?_____
_____

Write your own definition of consecration. _____
_____
_____

Daily Reflections: *Your Thoughts on Today's Study*

_____

_____

_____

_____

_____

_____

_____

_____

Prayer Journal: *Your Prayer on Today's Study*

_____

_____

_____

_____

_____

_____

_____

Chapter 5

Reviving the Heart

Psalm 138:7: *"Though I walk in the midst of trouble, thou wilt revive me: thou shalt stretch forth thine hand against the wrath of mine enemies, and thy right hand shall save me."*

So many things in this world seem to drain the very life out of us. Just the normal, menial tasks of life sometimes get overwhelming and begin to drain us. It's hard to imagine how people survive without God in their lives, but in reality, they are not surviving. They are living in Satan's temporary power. Without Christ as their Savior, they are dead in trespasses and sin. They are physically alive, yet spiritually dead. Only those who are alive in Christ are truly living.

Revival is for the living. You can't revive someone who was never alive. Revival means to resuscitate, to live again more vigorously.

The reason we all feel the need for a makeover is that we have lost our zeal. We no longer feel as anxious and vibrant as we once did. The simple act of living this life has taken its toll on us, and we feel about half dead.

"Revival means to resuscitate, to live again more vigorously."

Troubles of life have stripped us of our energy and motivation. We want to survive and overcome, but we feel lifeless and hopeless. In the midst of the daily grind, we have become preoccupied and hindered in our service to the Lord. We are operating with broken hearts, and we have no strength or desire to fight for survival. In our weakness we cry out to God, but our cry sounds something like this: "God, you said you would not put more on me than I could bear. God, you said you'd never leave me nor forsake me, so where are you? God, what about the part where you said you would bear my heavy load?" In our half-dead state of mind, we remember His promises, but we don't live in them.

Our Scripture text proves that if we live on God's Word and His promises then we can be resuscitated and revived. David said, "Though I walk in the midst of trouble, thou wilt revive me." David knew what it took to be revived, and he also knew what stripped him of that revival.

David blames his half-dead condition on his enemies. I don't believe David was just talking about our common enemy, Satan. I believe David called everything that drained or spiritually hindered him an enemy: Satan, friends, foes, physical ailments, political distress, fleshly battles, financial problems, relationships, family, work, church and the world.

David proclaimed revival for himself when he said, "Thou shalt stretch forth thine hand against the wrath of mine enemies, and thy right hand shall save me."

Revival for the heart requires a heart knowledge and wisdom of God's power in our lives. It requires an understanding of all we inherited when we became God's children. We have access to the throne of God, and we can boldly enter in and be revived in the Lord.

Reviving the heart requires:

- Atonement
- Assistance
- Abstinence
- Assurance
- Aspiration

I don't know what condition your heart is in, but I do know that without dependence upon God, we will not survive the storms of this life. Our hearts need mending because of our enemies. Let's allow God to repair us and make us over.

Day 1   *Atonement*

Romans 5:9-11: *"Much more then, being now justified by his blood, we shall be saved from wrath through him. [10]For if, when we were enemies, we were reconciled to God by the death of his Son, much more, being reconciled, we shall be saved by his life. [11]And not only so, but we also joy in God through our Lord Jesus Christ, by whom we have now received the atonement."*

This verse justifies our expectation to receive revival when we ask for it. We are guaranteed to be saved from wrath because we are justified by the blood of Jesus. We have been reconciled to God by the death of His only begotten.

We are to joy in the fact that we are at one with Christ, regardless of the condition of our hearts. Regardless of how far gone or half-dead we feel, our lifeline of hope is a right relationship with our Savior.

"Atonement means reconciliation of the guilty by divine sacrifice."

If you are born again, you have already received the atonement. You can have full fellowship with God, and you can experience revival. Atonement means reconciliation of the guilty by divine sacrifice. Jesus was your divine sacrifice, and through the salvation that made you alive, you can be revived in the hard times.

Atonement gives you:

- Access to the throne room.
- Forgiveness of your sins.
- Prayers that are heard and answered.
- Eternal life.
- Renewed life.
- Restoration.
- A relationship with God.

What has left you in need of revival? _____

_____

Have you cried out to God for help?_____

What is it you need God to do in your life right now? _____

_____

_____

Record Matthew 11:28-30 and memorize it. _____

_____

_____

_____

Daily Reflections: *Your Thoughts on Today's Study*

_____

_____

_____

_____

_____

_____

_____

_____

_____

Prayer Journal: *Your Prayer on Today's Study*

_____

_____

_____

_____

_____

_____

_____

_____

Day 2 *Assistance*

Psalm 138:7b: *"Thou shalt stretch forth thine hand against the wrath of mine enemies, and thy right hand shall save me."*

We've talked this week about being left in a half-dead state as Christians, unable to summon the strength to fight the good fight of faith. When we find ourselves in this condition, we must cry out for help. We must admit our weaknesses and allow someone to bind up our wounds. When David found himself half-dead, he cried out to God for divine assistance.

God is your divine assistance, too, just as He was for David. He is your rock and your fortress. He is your Great Physician. Psalm 33:20 says, "Our soul waiteth for the LORD: he *is* our help and our shield."

The Bible says again in Psalm 34:18, "The LORD *is* nigh unto them that are of a broken heart; and saveth such as be of a contrite spirit." When our hearts are broken, we only feel the pain. We bury ourselves in that pain, and we grow weaker and weaker in spirit. It is then that the enemy sneaks in to rob us of the hope and joy of who we are in Christ.

Dear scarred one, you need God's divine assistance in your life right now. Cry out to Him for deliverance. Let Him revive your heart so that you can be what He needs you to be for Him. God will be your divine assistance, but He also sends us other assistance in our trials and tribulations. That assistance comes in the form of our fellow man. The story of the Good Samaritan in Luke 10 is a demonstration of this principle.

The Good Samaritan stopped to assist the certain man on his way to Jericho when he was stripped, beaten and left half-dead. This certain man had left Jerusalem (the place of God) to go down to Jericho (a type of the world). This certain man was apparently looking for trouble, and he found it. Anytime we leave the things of God to venture out into the world, we can expect to be found half-dead spiritually. This is the reason we need revival!

The atonement we have in Christ Jesus is the reason we can ask for God's assistance. The way in which He chooses to send help is up to Him. We must be on guard at all times so that we don't miss that help when it comes. God will stretch forth His hand and save you.

In what area of your life do you need God's assistance?_____

_____

Have you previously or are you now overlooking God's divine assistance?___

_____

Has God sent a Good Samaritan your way? If so, who was it?_____

_____

Daily Reflections: *Your Thoughts on Today's Study*

_____

_____

_____

_____

_____

_____

_____

_____

_____

Prayer Journal: *Your Prayer on Today's Study*

_____

_____

_____

_____

_____

_____

_____

_____

Day 3   *Abstinence*

1 Thessalonians 5:22: *"Abstain from all appearance of evil."*

Abstinence means to refrain. Therefore, our Scripture text means that we should refrain from all appearance of evil. The world, our flesh and Satan have so much evil to offer us, corrupting our hearts toward God. We often give in to these temptations, and we find ourselves right in the center of evil.

We have been made alive in Christ Jesus. Our responsibility is to live in righteousness, untainted by the evil that surrounds us. Revival begins when we choose to deny the evil temptations thrown at us by the word, our flesh and Satan. We must learn to just say no! Peter said in 1 Peter 2:11, "Dearly beloved, I beseech *you* as strangers and pilgrims, abstain from fleshly lusts, which war against the soul."

The certain man on the Jericho road whom we studied about yesterday couldn't say no to the evil temptations that allured him. Most Christians have this same struggle, wanting to leave the things of God, if only temporarily, for the pleasures of this world. The Bible reminds us of the choices we must make in Hebrews 11:25: "Choosing rather to suffer affliction with the people of God, than to enjoy the pleasures of sin for a season."

One of the greatest steps toward reviving our hearts is being strong enough to say no to unrighteousness. Our assistance for saying no will come from the Lord. First Corinthians 10:13 says, "There hath no temptation taken you but such as is common to man: but God *is* faithful, who will not suffer you to be tempted above that ye are able; but will with the temptation also make a way to escape, that ye may be able to bear *it*."

You do not have to give in to temptation, desperation or defeat. God will make a way of escape so that you can abstain from evil.

What evil temptations are you being subjected to? _____
_____

Are you refraining from these temptations, or are you dabbling in them? _____
_____

How are these temptations and your responses affecting your Christian life? _
_____

Do you want God to make a way of escape?_____

Read 1 Peter 2:9-10 and record here what it says about you as a child of God.
_____

Daily Reflections: *Your Thoughts on Today's Study*

_____

_____

_____

_____

_____

_____

_____

_____

_____

Prayer Journal: *Your Prayer on Today's Study*

_____

_____

_____

_____

_____

_____

_____

_____

Day 4   *Assurance*

Isaiah 32:17: *"And the work of righteousness shall be peace; and the effect of righteousness quietness and assurance for ever."*

Do you know what assurance is? Assurance is the security of knowing that God lives inside of us and that nothing can ever separate us from His love. It is the security of knowing that our names are written in the Lambs book of life. These facts alone should cause us to break out in personal revival.

Our Scripture text teaches us that quietness and assurance are the effects of righteousness. Revival for the heart lies in righteousness. God is peace, joy and love. He is faith, meekness, and temperance. God is longsuffering, goodness and gentleness. Start living these things, and the assurance of revival will be within you.

It is a beautiful thing to know that we have the assurance of His presence in our lives. What a blessing to know that He hears us when we pray. He comforts us when we hurt. He supplies our every need. These are the assurances we have in Christ.

The most effective means of experiencing this assurance is to study the Word of God and believe what it says. Living the Word of God should never be an option; it should be our life.

I pray that you have the assurance of salvation. If you do not, let me invite you to receive Jesus as your personal Savior right now. Salvation is this simple: "Lord, I realize I am a sinner. Would you be my Savior?" Activate your faith in Jesus Christ. The Bible says in Ephesians 2:8-9, "For by grace are ye saved through faith; and that not of yourselves: *it is* the gift of God: [9]Not of works, lest any man should boast."

All who are lost can be made alive in Christ Jesus through salvation. Oh, what a blessed assurance to know that He is mine and I am His!

Do you need assurance in your heart about something? If so, list it here. _____
_____

Study the thing you need assurance of in the Bible and record here what God shows you about it. _____
_____
_____

"Blessed assurance – Jesus is mine. Oh, what a foretaste of glory divine."

Daily Reflections: *Your Thoughts on Today's Study*

_____

_____

_____

_____

_____

_____

_____

_____

Prayer Journal: *Your Prayer on Today's Study*

_____

_____

_____

_____

_____

_____

_____

Day 5   *Aspiration*

Psalm 85:6: *"Wilt thou not revive us again: that thy people may rejoice in thee?"*

Aspiration is the formal way to describe someone who is experiencing revival. The definition of aspiration is an exalted desire combined with holy zeal. Sounds like revival, doesn't it?

Our Scripture text asks the question, "With thou not revive us again?" Oh, yes, He will! God longs for His church to live exalted and holy. He longs to give us new desires, and He longs to see us spread those desires to others with joy and rejoicing.

It's easy to see when people are in personal revival. They shine like a diamond. They constantly share the things God is doing in their lives. They consistently study God's Word. You can see the Holy Spirit upon them. They look, walk and talk anointed.

If you have lost your zeal and desire to live for Jesus, then your heart needs revival. Search your heart today. Confess your condition to God.

"Aspiration is the formal way to describe someone who is experiencing revival."

You will find the symptoms of needing revival below. Do any of these fit your life?

- ☐ No joy
- ☐ No peace
- ☐ Constant worry
- ☐ Does not study the Word of God
- ☐ Feels abandoned by God
- ☐ Easily tempted
- ☐ Falls to temptation
- ☐ Harbors bitterness
- ☐ Easily finds fault in others
- ☐ Blames God
- ☐ Justifies their sin
- ☐ Murmurs and complains often
- ☐ Worldly

Maybe you're experiencing some of the many other symptoms of a need for revival. This is just a partial list. Allow God to reveal your need for revival to you. Remember, revival produces rejoicing, assurance and peace.

Did you find yourself to have any of the symptoms listed above? _____
_____

What do you intend to do about these symptoms? _____
_____

Find your aspiration in 1 Peter 3:10-11 and record what you learn here._____
_____

Daily Reflections: Your Thoughts on Today's Study

_____

_____

_____

_____

_____

_____

_____

_____

Prayer Journal: Your Prayer on Today's Study

_____

_____

_____

_____

_____

_____

_____

Chapter 6

Nursing the Wounds

Isaiah 53:5: *"But he was wounded for our transgressions, he was bruised for our iniquities: the chastisement of our peace was upon him; and with his stripes we are healed."*

I talk with and disciple the body of Christ daily. It breaks my heart when I hear them say that their wounds come mainly from other members of the family of God. What is even sadder is that we should expect it to be this way. The Bible says that if we reign with Christ, we shall also suffer with Him. Jesus was wounded for our transgressions, yet by His stripes we were healed.

"We can fully recover from the wounds of life."

How do we nurse our wounds? How do we get past the pain? How can we prevent being wounded again? We will discover the answers to these questions in this week's study on nursing our wounds. We will study:

- The bacteria
- The bitterness
- The bathing
- The balm
- The bandage

We can fully recover from the wounds of life. Jesus died so that we could be healed. Jesus was wounded for our transgressions. After resurrection He appeared to His disciples, His wounds were the evidence that He was the risen Savior. Let's not walk around wounded when such a dear price was paid for our healing!

The wounds that we acquire from the lessons of life can be the most beautiful part of our make over. Nurse your wounds under the care of the great Physician.

Day 1   *The Bacteria*

Romans 3:13: *"Their throat is an open sepulchre; with their tongues they have used deceit; the poison of asps is under their lips."*

Wounds require special care. Without proper care, wounds become infected and can lead to more serious complications. Bacteria forms in the wound, leading to dangerous, possibly life-threatening, conditions. If the bacterial infection is not stopped, it can spread into the bloodstream and cause infection throughout the whole body. Our Scripture text refers to this as poison.

In the spiritual sense of this subject, we have been wounded and poisoned by the effects of sin. Whether it's our own sin or the sins of others, sin has consequences. Those consequences can cause permanent damage in the lives of those who are affected by them if their wounds are not properly treated.

According to Scripture, we are all guilty of this bacteria called sin. Romans 3:10 says, "There is none righteous, no, not one." I don't know about you, friend, but I am ready to be free from the poisons of this life inflicted upon us by Satan, the flesh and the world. I have found the remedy, and I plan to take care of my wounds so that I can be an example of the healing brought about by the stripes of Jesus.

Isaiah 53:5 refers to healing of our sin when it says "with His stripes we are healed." Jesus became sin for us. Therefore, we can claim both healing of sin and deliverance from its poisons. Let's equip ourselves with the remedy so that we can conquer the growing bacteria in our lives.

The remedy for the poison of sin is:

- Trusting Christ as your Savior.
- Depending upon Him for all things.
- Forgiving as Christ forgives.
- Loving others with His love.
- Living in righteousness.
- Turning from our sin by turning to God.
- Controlling our tongues.
- Transforming our minds.

Choose one of these steps toward healing. Apply it to your wound and watch the changes start taking place.

Daily Reflections: Your Thoughts on Today's Study

_____

_____

_____

_____

_____

_____

_____

_____

_____

Prayer Journal: Your Prayer on Today's Study

_____

_____

_____

_____

_____

_____

_____

_____

Day 2   *The Bitterness*

Hebrews 12:14-15: *"Follow peace with all men, and holiness, without which no man shall see the Lord:* [15]*Looking diligently lest any man fail of the grace of God; lest any root of bitterness springing up trouble you, and thereby many be defiled."*

Bitterness is a root springing up to trouble you. Our healing may be slow to take place because of the bacteria of bitterness. Until we get rid of the root of our bacteria, our problems will continue and our wound will not heal.

We become discouraged and weary of the setbacks in our healing. Each time it appears that we are recuperating from our wounds, we have a relapse and find ourselves worse off than we were before. Naomi (in the book of Ruth) is an example of this.

Naomi's wounded heart was full of grief, anger and bitterness. She didn't like anyone, herself included, and she didn't want to be around anyone. She told her daughters-in-law to return to their mothers' homes. Then, Naomi changed her own name to Mara. Ruth 1:20-21 says, "And she said unto them, Call me not Naomi, call me Mara: for the Almighty hath dealt very bitterly with me. [21]I went out full, and the LORD hath brought me home again empty: why *then* call ye me Naomi, seeing the LORD hath testified against me, and the Almighty hath afflicted me?"

"Bitterness will place blame on God and hinder your fellowship with Him."

This story is such a parallel to our own behavior when a root of bitterness springs up in our lives. Bitterness produces anger and rebellion. It will cause you to accuse others of things they did not do. Bitterness will place blame on God and hinder your fellowship with Him.

Our bitterness can stem from years gone by or things that happened just today. If we don't deal with the issues that cause bitterness, they will fester up inside of us and rule our lives. Bitterness will defile both us and others around us ("lest any root of bitterness springing up trouble *you*, and thereby many be defiled").

Who is your bitterness wounding? Did you know that bitterness will become sin in your life? Bitterness will hurt your testimony, harden your heart and make you displeasing to God. It will surely make you over, but you will not be pleased with the outcome. No one will like the results of bitterness in your life.

I challenge you to confess your bitterness to God. Refuse to let it build poisons inside of you that you have no antidote for.

How can you overcome bitterness?

- Confess it to God.
- Deal with it in your heart and mind.
- Confront the person or thing that has caused your bitterness.
- Use it as part of your testimony.
- Pray for God to free you of the bitterness in your life.
- Have a desire to be rid of your bitterness.
- Stop blaming God.

Remember, by His stripes, this sin is healed.

Daily Reflections: *Your Thoughts on Today's Study*

_____

_____

_____

_____

_____

_____

_____

_____

_____

Prayer Journal: *Your Prayer on Today's Study*

_____

_____

_____

_____

_____

_____

_____

Day 3   *The Bathing*

1 John 1:7: *"But if we walk in the light, as he is in the light, we have fellowship one with another, and the blood of Jesus Christ his Son cleanseth us from all sin."*

Every wound that heals quickly and properly has had great care taken for it. Someone has taken extra precautions to make sure the wound was bathed frequently and cleansed with the appropriate solutions. The scar which is left by a wound often reveals the care that was taken in its healing. Large, unsightly scars are usually the result of improper care and neglect of the wound. Occasionally an unattractive wound is the byproduct of an unskilled surgeon, but more often than not, it is the result of neglect.

Our spiritual wounds must be cleansed and bathed in the blood of Jesus. If we try to cleanse them with any other solution, we are using the wrong stuff! Unless Jesus is our surgeon and primary care Physician, we will continue in our sickness.

Let's bathe ourselves in the glorious light of His love. Let's walk in the light as He is in the light. As we walk in fellowship with Christ, we will have fellowship with others. Our sins will all be cleansed by His blood.

When the blood of Jesus is applied, our wounds start closing up. As we mature in His grace, the scars start to fade and we begin to see the progress we've made in healing. Plead the blood over your situation and see what a difference it makes.

How long has it been since your wound was bathed in the blood of Jesus? ___
_____

Is your wound gaping, closing up or infected? _____
_____

Read 2 Corinthians 7:1 and record what you learned here._____
_____
_____

Daily Reflections: Your Thoughts on Today's Study

_____

_____

_____

_____

_____

_____

_____

_____

_____

Prayer Journal: *Your Prayer on Today's Study*

_____

_____

_____

_____

_____

_____

_____

_____

Day 4   *The Balm*

Jeremiah 8:22: *"Is there no balm in Gilead; is there no physician there? why then is not the health of the daughter of my people recovered?"*

The balm for our healing is the power of the Holy Spirit. If you have been born again, then the Holy Spirit lives inside of you. He is the ointment for your wounds. Our refusal to use the balm of God is a large part of the slow healing of our wounds. The Holy Spirit was given to us to bind us up in holiness and anoint us with His fresh oil.

The Holy Spirit will comfort you as He anoints you for God's service. We can also use several secondary balms in conjunction with the balm of the Spirit:

- The balm of prayer
- The balm of truth
- The balm of humility
- The balm of repentance

"The balm for our healing is the power of the Holy Spirit."

When we ask God for healing, it will come in His time and in His way. As we tend our wounds with humility, we soften the exterior so that the anointing can penetrate the sore. When we turn to God in repentance, we allow Him room to enter in and work through us in spite of our wounds.

Referring back to our Scripture text, we can see that the sin of the people was unable to be repaired. The balm was available, but no one was willing to apply it. God, help us not to refuse the leadership and the anointing of Your Holy Spirit. Teach us to apply truth to all areas of our lives. Teach us to cling to Jesus, our Healer.

Pray this prayer from your heart: "Oh, God, give me a willingness to recover from the illnesses of life. Show me the path of righteousness, and lead me in the way thereof. God, anoint my wounds with your Holy Spirit that I can receive the healing power of Jesus Christ. Thank you for Jesus and Calvary. Thank you for the balm of prayer. In Jesus' name. Amen."

Daily Reflections: *Your Thoughts on Today's Study*

_____

_____

_____

_____

_____

_____

_____

_____

Prayer Journal: *Your Prayer on Today's Study*

_____

_____

_____

_____

_____

_____

_____

Day 5   The Bandage

Luke 10:34: *"And went to him, and bound up his wounds, pouring in oil and wine, and set him on his own beast, and brought him to an inn, and took care of him."*

Here we are again studying the certain man who fell among thieves on his way to Jericho. All of those who were labeled as righteous had passed him by. The priest and the Levite went by without helping him in any way. But the Scripture says that a certain Samaritan went to him and bound up his wounds. Not only did the Samaritan bind him up, but he poured oil and wine into his wounds. The Samaritan knew how to properly care for this man's wounds. He didn't just put a band-aid on him and carry on. The Samaritan cared enough to take the precautions against infection we discussed earlier in the week.

The oil and wine poured on the certain man's wounds represented cleansing and anointing. Taking this analogy a step farther, the Good Samaritan is a representative of Jesus Christ and His compassion toward us.

As we follow the actions of the Good Samaritan we see that his care for the certain man did not stop with the bandaging and anointing of his wounds. He picked this certain man up, took him to an inn, and took care of him. Sounds just like Jesus, doesn't it? Still, the Good Samaritan, before departing the next day, gave money to the host to continue taking care of the wounded man then said, "Take care of him; and whatsoever thou spendest more, when I come again, I will repay thee."

The bandaging of the Good Samaritan went a long way. I feel sure the wounded man experienced a makeover from the inside out. Once, we fell among thieves. We, too, were stripped, wounded and left half-dead. Jesus passed by, bandaged us with His unconditional and eternal love, paid all of our sin debt and took care of us. Jesus is still applying bandages to our open and infected wounds. He is doing a new work in our lives. May this new work in us bandage the lives of those who have fallen among thieves.

Do you know someone with whom you could share the compassion of the Good Samaritan? If so, who is it? _____

_____

Are you willing to not only bandage the wounds of another, but to also apply cleanser and balm, put them up and pay their way? _____

What is God saying to us in 2 Corinthians 4:1? Write the verse here: _____

_____

_____

Record and memorize Galatians 6:2._____

_____

_____

Daily Reflections: Your Thoughts on Today's Study

_____

_____

_____

_____

_____

_____

_____

_____

Prayer Journal: Your Prayer on Today's Study

_____

_____

_____

_____

_____

_____

_____

Chapter 7

Overcoming the Pain

Romans 8:22: *"For we know that the whole creation groaneth and travaileth in pain together until now."*

*P*ain takes many forms: physical, mental, emotional and spiritual. Physical pain can be masked or relieved by simply taking a pain pill. It can be totally alleviated by pinpointing its cause and finding a cure. The cure may require treatments or even surgery, but in most cases it will go away.

Mental and emotional pains are often treated with medications, but the pain of the circumstances remains, preventing a healing. These pains can be caused by things that happened in our childhood or just by the general stress of life. The effects of mental and emotional pain usually cause physical pain as well. The stress of circumstances can cause many physical ailments: chest pain, headaches, heart palpitations, stomach upset and much more. The release of stress hormones into the body affects the whole nervous system.

We can mask mental and emotional pain with nerve pills, antidepressants, HRT, sleeping pills or even the most drastic measures of street drugs, alcohol and tobacco. Regardless of the category our pain falls into, it will affect us spiritually if it goes unattended.

"Whatever diversities of pain you're carrying, God will help you."

Our first goal is to find the cause of our pain. It can be anything: rejection, abuse, divorce, abandonment, finances, disappointments, fears, addictions, relationships, our past, feelings of failure, etc... After we identify the cause of our pain, we must confront it and deal with it. The longer we mask it the more damage it will cause.

Harboring pain builds a resistance for healing. Even physical discomfort seems easier to handle when we can complain. Though it doesn't take the pain away, there's just something soothing in being able to admit that you're hurting.

After we've identified, confronted and dealt with our pain, we must confess to God its effects. God will help us to deal with the pain, and He will deliver us from its bondage. He is our only hope for overcoming the pains of this life. He can restore us physically, mentally, emotionally and spiritually.

Whatever diversities of pain you're carrying, God will help you. We read of so many people throughout the Bible's pages who lived lives of dreaded pain. They suffered from sin sickness, physical ailments, mental adversities, emotional breakdowns and spiritual warfare. God was faithful to see them through, and He is the same God now that He was then. He will see you through the pain you're carrying.

Our Scripture text teaches us that all creation has groanings, and we will all travail in pain, but we have overcoming power in Christ. We must be willing to:

- Feel the pain.
- Face the pain.
- Funnel the pain.
- Fight the pain.
- Forget the pain.

When we come to Christ with a willingness to be made better, He will do a makeover in our lives. That makeover starts from the inside and works its way out, and when it's complete you'll know that you'll never be the same again. God will heal your pain, and you will become a stronger Christian.

Day 1   *Feel the Pain*

Hebrews 4:15: *"For we have not an high priest which cannot be touched with the feeling of our infirmities; but was in all points tempted like as we are, yet without sin."*

Jesus Christ hung on Calvary and died a cruel death for all the world. He was tortured and beaten. He was crowned with thorns, despised and rejected. He bled; He hurt; His body was mutilated and He felt every agonizing blow. He was beaten, spat upon, and whipped with a cat-of-nine-tails, and He felt every stinging pain. Yes, Jesus was so much man that He, too, felt physical pain that led to emotional, mental and spiritual infirmities. His pain could not be denied. Jesus had to suffer for the sin of the world, and nothing would be able to mask His pain.

My friend, you must feel your pain, too. Regardless of its type, pain is inevitable. We will suffer, and we will hurt. We can live in denial of our pain, but it will eventually become too overwhelming to deny. It will begin to control you thinking and your behavior. Even your countenance will change. Pain has a debilitating effect on our lives.

"God will be faithful to help us as we allow ourselves to feel the pain and identify its cause."

We can draw the following conclusions from our pain:

1. Pain tells us there is an underlying problem.
2. We must pinpoint that problem.
3. Masking the pain is only a temporary fix.
4. We must pursue a permanent solution to not only kill the pain but to heal its cause.

God will be faithful to help us as we allow ourselves to feel the pain and identify its cause. Our Scripture text tells us that Jesus is touched with the feelings of our infirmities. He cares about our pain. He knows it makes us weak and mentally and emotionally fragile.

Jesus has experienced every pain that you now feel. Therefore, you can go to Him for comfort and healing. Take your pain to Jesus. He understands. He knows you are hurting. Reflect back on Calvary. Remember the critical suffering He went through for you. Allow Him to help your infirmities. Confess the problem to Jesus Christ, Savior of the world:

I confess that my pain is:

- ☐ Physical
- ☐ Mental
- ☐ Emotional
- ☐ Spiritual
- ☐ Other
- ☐ All of the above

My pain causes me to be:

- ☐ Bitter
- ☐ Weak
- ☐ Rebellious
- ☐ Angry
- ☐ Weary
- ☐ Afraid
- ☐ Confused
- ☐ Restless
- ☐ Hopeless
- ☐ Doubtful
- ☐ Faithless
- ☐ Hurting

Challenge yourself to research your pain in the Bible. Find someone or something that relates to you and what you are going through. As you realize that you are not alone, you will be able to feel your pain and deal with it. The process of healing will make you feel like a brand new person.

Daily Reflections: *Your Thoughts on Today's Study*

_____

_____

_____

_____

_____

_____

_____

_____

Prayer Journal: *Your Prayer on Today's Study*

_____

_____

_____

_____

_____

_____

_____

Day 2   *Face the Pain*

Hebrews 4:15: *"For we have not an high priest which cannot be touched with the feeling of our infirmities; but was in all points tempted like as we are, yet without sin."*

Yesterday we discussed the first part of this verse as we allowed ourselves to feel the pain in our lives. Today we will cover the complete verse as we face our pain.

Facing our pain requires us to examine the effects it has had on our lives. If you'll notice, our text says that Jesus was in all points tempted like as we are, yet without sin. Pain will cause us to separate ourselves from fellowship with God through sin.

Pain can come from any number of sources, but God allows it to test us. The word tempted in our text means to be tested, proved and disciplined. Jesus was tested and proved, and He was found very disciplined. The text says "yet without sin." Jesus faced His pain.

Whether our pain is physical, mental, emotional or spiritual, we must face it like Jesus faced His pain. When we study the word "face," it explains itself. In the verb tense, it means to stand before, to confront, to meet bravely or boldly; it means to oppose and resist; to face a challenge. Jesus faced His challenge. His pain was the sin of the world, and He bravely stood before His accusers, opposing, resisting and confronting His pain.

As Jesus faced the pain of Calvary, He fell into every category of hurt. From physical to spiritual, Jesus suffered and conquered it all. He could have called a legion of angels. He could have backed out long before the journey began. But He didn't. He stood strong and faced the agony of it all so that you and I could have the strength to face our pain.

We can only face and conquer our pain when Jesus is our Savior. Regardless of what you are going through, you can confront and oppose your agony through the power of Jesus Christ. Philippians 4:13 says, "I can do all things through Christ which strengtheneth me." We have no need to run and hide. We do not need to mask our pain with addictions to painkillers, alcohol, tobacco, etc…God will aid you in your times of pain. He will help you to cope in your times of weakness.

In your physical pain, God will direct you to the proper physician who can find the root of your pain. He will provide someone who can prescribe the medication for the cause of the pain.

In you mental and emotional pain, God will direct you to someone you can talk to about your feelings, someone who will point you to God as the solution. He will lead you to the truths of His Word that can transform and heal your mental and emotional pain. God has also given us psychologists and counselors to help with mental and emotional pain.

In your spiritual pain, He will make Himself real to you. He will show up in a way that you cannot deny His presence, love and provision for you. God's prescription for our spiritual pain is transforming the mind by reading and studying His Word. We must go to Him in prayer daily. Have faith in God's promises, and trust that He will do what He says.

Are you facing your pain?_____

_____

If you're not facing your pain, how are you masking it? _____

_____

Like Jesus, are you facing your pain without sin? _____

_____

Daily Reflections: Your Thoughts on Today's Study

_____

_____

_____

_____

_____

_____

_____

_____

Prayer Journal: Your Prayer on Today's Study

_____

_____

_____

_____

_____

_____

_____

Day 3   *Funnel the Pain*

1 Chronicles 4:9: *"And Jabez was more honourable than his brethren: and his mother called his name Jabez, saying, Because I bare him with sorrow."*

Funneling the pain refers to preventing spillage. The purpose of a funnel is to prevent things from spilling. How many times have you tried to transfer liquids from one container to another without a funnel? What happens? You usually end up spilling stuff all over the place, doing more harm than good.

In our Scripture text, we see that Jabez' mother was facing some sort of pain. She said, "I bare him with sorrow." Her pain spilled over into the life of her son. Can you imagine your mother naming you after her pain? How do you think the effects of her pain spilled over into the life of her child?

If you've studied the prayer of Jabez (1 Chronicles 4:10), you know that he did not want to live the definition of his name. He prayed, "Oh that thou wouldest bless me indeed, and enlarge my coast, and that thine hand might be with me, and that thou wouldest keep *me* from evil, that it may not grieve me! And God granted him that which he requested."

Jabez funneled not only the sorrow in which he was born but also the curse of that sorrow that sought to spill over into his own life. He funneled the pain of his family by crying out to God for blessing and deliverance. And, God granted his request.

"God is the ultimate caregiver when we hurt."

We, too, can funnel our pain, whether it is generational or circumstantial. We can cry out to God. We can make Him our funnel for pain. When we allow Him to carry our pain, it will not spill over into the lives of others.

Jabez knew that God had something better than a life of sorrow to offer him. Just because his mother bore him in sorrow didn't mean that he had to live in sorrow. Similarly, just because we must feel and face our pain, that doesn't mean that our pain must spill over into the lives of others. It is often said that hurting people hurt people, but think how much of this hurt could be stopped if we would only funnel our pain into the hands of God.

The Word of God teaches us to go to the Lord in our times of need. God is the ultimate caregiver when we hurt. He will reveal the source of our pain, and will take the hurt away. He is the funnel and the physician for all of our afflictions.

Let's take a look at some the hurting people in the Bible who funneled their pain into God's hands:

Psalm 25:18: David cried. "Look upon mine affliction and my pain; and forgive all my sins."

Jeremiah 15:18: Jeremiah said, "Why is my pain perpetual, and my wound incurable, *which* refuseth to be healed?"

2 Corinthians 11:27: Paul made this statement: "In weariness and painfulness, in watchings often, in hunger and thirst, in fastings often, in cold and nakedness."

If you were to funnel your pain into the hands of God, what would your cry be? _____

_____

_____

You can funnel your pain into God's control. If you answered the above question, you have already confessed your pain. Are you willing to allow God to help you? _____

_____

_____

Looking back on your pain, how many people have been affected by your spillage? Who are they?_____

_____

_____

Record Revelation 21:4. _____

_____

_____

Is your pain past, present, or perpetual? _____

_____

_____

Funnel your pain into the throne room of God and leave it there.

Daily Reflections: Your Thoughts on Today's Study

_____

_____

_____

_____

_____

_____

_____

_____

_____

Prayer Journal: *Your Prayer on Today's Study*

_____

_____

_____

_____

_____

_____

_____

Day 4   *Fight the Pain*

1 Chronicles 4:10: *"And Jabez called on the God of Israel, saying, Oh that thou wouldest bless me indeed, and enlarge my coast, and that thine hand might be with me, and that thou wouldest keep me from evil, that it may not grieve me! And God granted him that which he requested."*

Yesterday we discussed the life of Jabez a man who was born in sorrow. As we review his life again today, we must see him as a man who knew how to fight his sorrow. Jabez could have allowed his mother's pain to control everything about his life. He could have rested in self-pity and misfortune. He could have accepted the family curse. He could have chosen a life of depression and constant hardships. He could have chosen negativity and poverty and lived a life of total defeat, but he chose to fight for a more blessed life.

As we dissect our Scripture text for today, we see the armor that he put on to overcome his pain:

- He called on the God of Israel.
- He asked for God to bless him.
- He asked for his life to be enlarged.
- He asked for God's hand to guide him.
- He asked for God's protection from evil.

The greatest weapon in our warfare with adversities is turning to God. This was Jabez' first response to his pain. Turning to God is the key to overcoming our pain. We cannot win the battles of this life without God's power. Jabez could not have overcome the sorrow into which he was born without recognizing God's power.

Part of the reason we can't overcome our hurts today is that we refuse to turn to God. We turn to everyone and everything else instead. We give in to our pain rather than fighting to overcome.

Some examples are found in the Bible of people who stopped fighting their pain:

- Naomi: She was so defeated that she changed her name to mean bitter. She experienced mental and emotional pain.
- Eve: She became so defeated that she gave in to the lies of the devil. She experienced physical and spiritual pain.
- Gomer: Gomer was so defeated that she gave in to the family curse of sexual immorality. She experience spiritual and emotional pain.

These women were defeated in their circumstances. Unlike Jabez, they sat down in their anxiety and gave up on God.

My friend, if we choose to dwell in our pain, we too will find ourselves bitter, confused and defeated. We must fight the good fight of faith. When you look in the mirror, don't see yourself as broken and defeated. See who you are when you're empowered by God to fight the battle. See yourself clothed in the whole armor of God.

Review you life as a Christian. Evaluate your defense mechanisms. Allow God to build you up in Him. Allow Him to bless your life with victory. Romans 8:32 says, "What shall we then say to these things? If God *be* for us, who *can be* against us?"

Isaiah 35:3-4 says, "Strengthen ye the weak hands, and confirm the feeble knees. [4]Say to them *that are* of a fearful heart, Be strong, fear not: behold, your God will come *with* vengeance, *even* God *with* a recompense; he will come and save you."

God wants us to fight our pain by standing with the Sword of the Lord in hand. God promises our victory and deliverance through Him. Whether our pain is physical, mental, emotional or spiritual, God will come and fight for us, and He will save us.

What happens when we stop fighting?

- We grow weaker each day.
- We allow the disease to control us.
- We set ourselves up for deception.
- We fall for anything.
- We find ourselves feeling totally defeated.
- We find ourselves doing unhealthy things.

Let's use Jabez as our example and get back to fighting our pain. Let's use the same defenses against pain that Jabez used:

- The presence of God.
- The blessing of God.
- The provision of God.
- The guidance of God.
- The protection of God.

When we clothe ourselves with these five defenses, like Jabez, we will find our requests granted.

Which of these five defenses are you without?_____

_____

Which of these do you feel you most need to overcome your pain? _____

_____

You can have these defenses just by asking for them. Make your request to God here._____

Daily Reflections: Your Thoughts on Today's Study

_____

_____

_____

_____

_____

_____

_____

_____

Prayer Journal: Your Prayer on Today's Study

_____

_____

_____

_____

_____

_____

_____

Day 5   *Forgetting the Pain*

Philippians 3:13: *"Brethren, I count not myself to have apprehended: but this one thing I do, forgetting those things which are behind, and reaching forth unto those things which are before."*

We have dealt all week with the diversities, causes and effects of pain. We have received answers and solutions to overcoming the toils of life. We must now make a decision: will we overcome our pain?

The only way to truly overcome our pain is to deal with every facet of pain that has penetrated our life and then forget it. God can only heal the hearts of those who truly want healing. If we choose to dwell in the pain, then we have chosen the pain over God. We have chosen to live a life of defeat.

Our Scripture text was penned by the apostle Paul. Paul suffered perpetually in every facet of pain. Physical, mental, emotional and spiritual pain chased him wherever he went, but he never quit and gave up on God. He never got angry with God, and he never allowed his pain to spill over into the lives of those around him. He didn't give in to addictions or defeat. Instead, he overcame his pain.

"God can only heal the hearts of those who truly want healing."

Paul proclaimed his victory in today's Scripture text. He did not allow his pain to defeat him. Like Jabez, Paul faced his pain, felt his pain for Christ's sake, funneled his pain through an intimate relationship with God, and then fought his pain by living the Word of God. That's why Paul could boldly proclaim that he was forgetting his pain by reaching forth unto those things which were before.

In paraphrase, Paul was saying, "Hey, reach for God. He is before you. Stop dwelling in the pain. From this moment forward, your pain falls into the past. Forget those things which are behind." Regardless of how painful our lives have been, we can start new right now. We can bury the pains of life, and we can move forward in Christ Jesus.

The key to forgetting our pain is remembering that God is before us. He is available to help us overcome our pain. Before means in front of, at hand, or close enough to touch. God is within your reach. Are you ready to forget your pain and move on in your relationship with God and others? Until you are ready to overcome your pain, it will control your whole life. Regardless of how much we feel, face, fight and funnel our pain, forgetting it is the only way to overcome it.

How do we forget our pain?

- Realize that the pain did not take your life.
- Find the positive rather than the negative in your pain.
- Admit that you learned something through your pain.
- Understand that God loves you, and He is there to see you through.
- Use your pain to help someone else who is hurting.
- Talk to someone you trust about your pain.

The healing process begins to take effect as we forget our pain. We start to feel and act better. We begin to realize that life is much better without the pain. Like Paul, we start to reach for the things ahead. We become new as the healing begins to restore our joy. We become motivated to be all that we can be for God. Soon, everyone around us begins to notice the changes in our lives.

Forgetting the pain will also free us from the battle inside. We begin to think differently and to view life with a whole new perspective.

I pray that you are ready to forget your pain. I don't know how your pain has affected your life, but I do know what it can cause. I pray that you have freed yourself from something that seems to control everything about you. Pain is a very difficult battle to fight. It will make you someone you never thought you could be.

Do you love yourself and God enough to forget your pain? _____

_____

Have you identified your pain through these past few days of study? If so, record your pain here. _____

_____

_____

Study Revelation 21:3-8. Record here what you learned from this Scripture about overcoming and forgetting your pain. _____

_____

_____

_____

Daily Reflections: *Your Thoughts on Today's Study*

_____

_____

_____

_____

_____

_____

_____

_____

_____

Prayer Journal: *Your Prayer on Today's Study*

_____

_____

_____

_____

_____

_____

_____

Chapter 8

The Healing Process

Matthew 9:35: *"And Jesus went about all the cities and villages, teaching in their synagogues, and preaching the gospel of the kingdom, and healing every sickness and every disease among the people."*

Regardless of what sickness may be upon you, Jesus is the divine healer. You will not find a place in Scripture where He refused to help those seeking deliverance, no matter what their affliction was. From sin sickness to physical sickness, Jesus has the power to heal every disease.

Examples of diverse healings are found throughout the Bible. Naaman was healed of leprosy. Hannah was healed of barrenness. Naomi was healed of depression. In the Gospels, Jesus healed a hemorrhaging woman, a man possessed with devils, two blind men, an epileptic boy, a man with dropsy, a bowed woman. Jesus also healed a man with an unclean spirit, a son with fever, and a paralytic. God is faithful to heal all kinds of sickness.

The Word of God teaches us that He is no respecter of persons. Therefore, we can believe that the Great Physician who healed all those afflicted in ancient times still heals those who are afflicted today.

"God knows the sickness that you are fighting today."

Our Scripture text says that Jesus went about healing every sickness and every disease among the people. However, we must not overlook a very important thing that took place in this particular process of healing. The text says that Jesus "went about all the cities and villages, teaching in their synagogues, and preaching the gospel of the kingdom." Jesus' process of healing was to teach the truth and the good news of eternal life as He healed those who passed by

Him. Healing was also taking place in hearts as He taught and preached. Physical, mental, emotional and spiritual healing was performed in the lives of all who heard, received and believed in the power of Jesus Christ.

God knows the sickness that you are fighting today. He is ever present in the lives of His children. Healing for your sin-sickness took place at the moment of salvation. Jesus Christ Himself took your place and died for your disease of iniquity.

I realize that many today do not receive the divine healings that were performed in biblical times. Daily, we see people dying with cancer, Alzheimer's, tumors, etc... I don't have the answers for these things, but I know Someone who does. As we sit with Him in Heaven for an eternity, Jesus will explain these mysteries to us.

This week, we will study the process of serving God in spite of the prolonged and possibly terminal diseases we must face. Divine healing may not come, but spiritual healing is our source of power for enduring afflictions of the body, soul and mind.

My testimony of healing first involved spiritual healing. I realized that healing in my relationship with Him was necessary, even if He never healed me of the seizures, if He never healed my finances, and if He never healed my marriage. The healing process had to start with me. I had to first allow God to remove the sickness of rebellion, anger and sin from my life. I was angry with Him, I was rebellious as a Christian, and I was drowning in the effects of my lifestyle.

My healing began first with repentance, then with confession. I fell so in love with Jesus that physical healing no longer mattered. God showed me that I must learn of Him. I had to allow Him to heal my mind and my thinking. He revealed to me that whether or not He chose to heal my body, I had to love Him and use my seizures for His glory.

The closer I grew in my relationship to God, the more I began to feel as though I was already healed. The Great Physician became my strength to endure them. He became the balm for my pain. I began to understand Romans 8:28: "And we know that all things work together for good to them that love God, to them who are the called according to *his* purpose."

I purposed in my heart to use my sickness for the glory of God. I became so focused on Him during this process that one day, after a while, I found my finances healed, my marriage healed, and I have now been seizure free for more than 15 years! God is so good!

We all must abide in the healing process mentioned in our Scripture text. We must learn of Him, be taught by Him, receive Him as Savior and believe whatever He says. The next phase of healing comes from within. We must:

- Be determined.
- Be disciplined.
- Be dependent.
- Be defensive.
- Be delivered.

Day 1   *Be Determined*

Luke 8:43-44: *"And a woman having an issue of blood twelve years, which had spent all her living upon physicians, neither could be healed of any, [44]Came behind him, and touched the border of his garment: and immediately her issue of blood stanched."*

For twelve years, this hemorrhaging woman had spent her time and money trying to find a cure for her disease. The only hope she found was in the healing power of Jesus Christ. When she heard that Jesus was coming to town, she became determined to do whatever she had to do to get to Him. When the Healer arrived, a crowd had gathered, but with determination, she pressed through to Him. Her determination to be healed was so great that she knew just touching the hem of His garment would be enough to make her whole.

My friend, determination worked for this lady. Jesus immediately acknowledged that someone had touched Him. The woman came trembling and falling down before Him to confess that she was the one who had touched Him. She also came proclaiming healing! Her determination to believe that Jesus was the healer brought victory in her life.

Determination is the key factor in the process of healing. Too often, we give up just before deliverance comes. We allow pressures, pains and persecutions to overcome our faith in God. Like Peter when he walked on the water, we start out walking toward Jesus, but we start sinking in our circumstances just before we reach Him. Feelings of weakness and defeat overtake us, and we miss the blessing that God intended for us to enjoy.

The woman with the issue of blood is a great example of determination. All it takes to endure times of affliction is a consistent faith in God. Pressing through the circumstances that weaken you and standing on the promises of God's Word will get you through your darkest hour.

Determination requires action. You must put forth an effort to overcome your sickness. You cannot wallow in your illness. Regardless of your ailment, you must fight to become well. Determination means getting up when you fall. If you stay down, you'll only grow weaker, and the enemy will attack and leave you wounded. The enemy wants to destroy your determination to overcome. Healing is a long and painful road when you have no energy to fight the battle.

Are you at a point where you are about to give up in your fight for healing? Do you feel that you just can't take anymore? Perhaps the crowd appears too great for you to press through. Don't give up just before touching the hem of His garment. Reach out before you give up; Jesus is so near. Deliverance is before you. Be determined to overcome.

Can you identify your sickness? Circle the ones that best relate to you:

Sin sickness   Marital Sickness   Physical Sickness

Financial sickness   Emotional Sickness   Spiritual Sickness

Mental sickness   other

Have you already given up?_____

_____

How long has this sickness plagued you? _____

_____

Do you control the sickness, or does it control you?_____

_____

Do you want to be delivered? _____

_____

What does Malachi 4:2-3 say about healing? _____

_____

Daily Reflections: Your Thoughts on Today's Study

_____

_____

_____

_____

_____

_____

_____

_____

_____

Prayer Journal: Your Prayer on Today's Study

_____

_____

_____

_____

_____

_____

_____

_____

Day 2   *Be Disciplined*

John 5:5-6: *"And a certain man was there, which had an infirmity thirty and eight years. ⁶When Jesus saw him lie, and knew that he had been now a long time in that case, he saith unto him, Wilt thou be made whole?"*

This man in our Scripture text sought healing for 30 years. Every season, he lay by the pool waiting for the waters to be stirred by the angel. Each opportunity he had to step into the water was thwarted by others who could move faster than he. Still, he kept putting forth the effort to make his way into the pool. He was slow, and he was beaten by the pace of others, but he was disciplined enough to keep trying.

Discipline requires us to keep trying. As we keep ourselves right with God, we will begin to see Him working in our lives. Your discipline will draw Him to you and your need, just as this man's discipline drew Jesus to him.

The discipline that brings healing is the discipline of a consistent, personal relationship with God. It is persistence in the pursuit of righteousness. The man who waited by the pool of Bethesda was persistent in being there, and he continuously pursued getting into the water. Discipline is the reason he was found faithful and received healing.

"The discipline that brings healing is the discipline of a consistent, personal relationship with God."

We don't know this man's infirmity; maybe no one else knows yours. But, we do know that God honors those who trust Him, depend upon Him and wait for Him. He honors a heart of faithfulness even when afflictions seem more than we can bear.

God expects us to remain disciplined in service, Bible study, prayer and holiness. These things contribute to our healing process. We must remain faithful to God, and He will be faithful to us.

Have your afflictions overcome your discipline? _____

_____

Are you struggling with any of the following areas of faithfulness? If so, circle the ones you need to concentrate on:

Prayer   Bible Study   Righteousness
Service   All of these

According to Daniel 6:10, in which area was Daniel disciplined?_____
_____

What happened to Daniel because of his discipline? _____
_____

Regardless of our afflictions, we must be disciplined.

Daily Reflections: Your Thoughts on Today's Study

_____

_____

_____

_____

_____

_____

_____

_____

_____

Prayer Journal: Your Prayer on Today's Study

_____

_____

_____

_____

_____

_____

_____

Day 3   *Be Dependent*

John 15:5: *"I am the vine, ye are the branches: He that abideth in me, and I in him, the same bringeth forth much fruit: for without me ye can do nothing."*

We can go to physicians, we can take medications, we can follow every doctor's order precisely, but until we come under the care of the Great Physician, complete healing will not happen.

Our text says that Jesus is the vine and we are the branches. The only way a branch can survive and bear fruit is by abiding in the vine. This is a beautiful analogy of our relationship with Christ and the dependence upon Him that He expects from us.

Abiding in Jesus gives us His strength and power to function in this life. We will bear fruits of righteousness as long as we depend upon the Lord. As our text says, "Without (Jesus) ye can do nothing."

As we study this analogy further, we see that the branch not only survives, but it grows and matures in the vine. As long as it is grafted to the vine, the branch can withstand seasonal changes. As we depend upon God, we, too, will face seasonal changes. As long as we abide in Him, we can withstand these changes, as painful as they may be.

"Through all of life's pain, heartaches and sickness, we find our power for survival in being grafted into Jesus."

Ecclesiastes 3:1-8 says:

> To every *thing there is* a season, and a time to every purpose under the heaven: [2]A time to be born, and a time to die; a time to plant, and a time to pluck up *that which is* planted; [3]A time to kill, and a time to heal; a time to break down, and a time to build up; [4]A time to weep, and a time to laugh; a time to mourn, and a time to dance; [5]A time to cast away stones, and a time to gather stones together; a time to embrace, and a time to refrain from embracing; [6]A time to get, and a time to lose; a time to keep, and a time to cast away; [7]A time to rend, and a time to sew; a time to keep silence, and a time to speak; [8]A time to love, and a time to hate; a time of war, and a time of peace.

We can endure all of these seasons of change as long as we remain dependent upon the vine. Through all of life's pain, heartaches and sickness, we find our power for survival in being grafted into Jesus.

It can be difficult to depend on God when we feel that He has abandoned us in our pain. We are not prepared to cling to the vine in the face of unforeseen adversity. How can we continue to trust in the God who allowed this pain? The answer is found in His Word. In these times of trouble, we must apply ourselves to reading and studying His holy book. We will begin to hear His voice, receive His instructions and cling to His promises. And we will discover that we are clinging to the only One who can deliver us.

Jesus, who never changes, is your Great Physician. Through His Word, He will prescribe the antidote for your disease. He will not perform physical reconstructive surgery, but He will make you new on the inside. Healing will come to your life if you follow His instructions and remain under His care. It may not be the healing your flesh longs for, but it will be the healing your heart needs.

When we learn to accept God's plan for healing, we have truly become dependent upon Him. Without Him, we can do nothing.

Depending on God requires:

- Complete trust in His Word.
- A life of total faith in Him.
- A love for God above all others.

Are you struggling with one of these requirements? If so, which one? _____
_____

In what area of your life do you need to depend on God right now? _____
_____

What types of sickness has this need created for you? _____
_____

What does Philippians 4:19 mean to you?_____
_____

Daily Reflections: Your Thoughts on Today's Study

_____

_____

_____

_____

_____

_____

_____

_____

_____

Prayer Journal: Your Prayer on Today's Study

_____

_____

_____

_____

_____

_____

_____

_____

Day 4   Be Defensive

1 Peter 3:15: *"But sanctify the Lord God in your hearts: and be ready always to give an answer to every man that asketh you a reason of the hope that is in you with meekness and fear."*

How many times have you been down and found a source of survival that shed a ray of hope on your situation? How many times has that hope been shot down by someone or something? We have many enemies who seek to shatter our hope and rejoicing.

So far, we've learned this week that we must be determined, disciplined and dependent upon God in order for healing to take place in our lives. In order to stand in these things, we must be defensive in our walk with God. In order to be defensive against the negative tactics of the world, our flesh and Satan, we must arm ourselves with the armor of God.

Our Scripture text tells us to sanctify the Lord God in our hearts. This means allowing Him to rule over our hearts and minds. We equip ourselves to be on the defense and prepare ourselves to give an answer for the hope that is in us by setting ourselves apart from the evil influences of the world and Satan.

"The enemy is great and powerful. He is allowed to sift us at times, but he is not allowed to destroy us."

The hope we have comes only from God. We must protect that hope from being shot down by the enemy. This is the next step in equipping ourselves for defense. Our protective apparel is found in Ephesians 6:10-18. Verse 11 says, "Put on the whole armour of God, that ye may be able to stand against the wiles of the devil." Verse 12 teaches us who our enemies are: principalities, powers, rulers of darkness of this world, and spiritual wickedness in high places. Verses 14-18 list our armor:

- Gird your loins with truth.
- Put on the breastplate of righteousness.
- Have your feet shod with the gospel of peace.
- Take the shield of faith.
- Put on the helmet of salvation.
- Carry the Sword of the Spirit (the Word of God).
- Pray.
- Watch (be on guard).
- Have perseverance.
- Be in supplication for all saints.

With this armor, we should be able to defend our hearts against the fiery darts of the wicked. We are responsible for staying on the defense. We must always be ready to fight. We must be so equipped and prepared for the fight that the weapons that come against us cannot shatter the hope that is within us.

Being defensive requires us to stand on truth, demonstrate righteousness, walk in peace, live by faith, receive salvation, and commit the Word of God to our hearts and minds. If we fail to abide in these, then we can expect defeat. Our hope will be deterred, and healing will be delayed.

The enemy is great and powerful. He is allowed to sift us at times, but he is not allowed to destroy us. He can wound us and strip us, but only if we don't fight back. The moment we put on our apparel, his weapons start to ricochet off of us and backfire onto him.

Which piece of armor have you left off, causing your hope to be shattered?___

_____

Which weapons is the enemy using against you? Lies? Deception? The world? Your flesh? _____

_____

Take time right now to memorize one Scripture that you can use as a weapon against your enemies today. Record that Scripture here. _____

_____

_____

_____

Daily Reflections: Your Thoughts on Today's Study

_____

_____

_____

_____

_____

_____

_____

_____

Prayer Journal: *Your Prayer on Today's Study*

_____

_____

_____

_____

_____

_____

_____

_____

Day 5   *Be Delivered*

Psalm 34:17-19: *"The righteous cry, and the LORD heareth, and delivereth them out of all their troubles. [18]The LORD is nigh unto them that are of a broken heart; and saveth such as be of a contrite spirit. [19]Many are the afflictions of the righteous: but the LORD delivereth him out of them all."*

Deliverance is the final process in our healing. This refers to divine healing and deliverance from the strongholds that our ailments have placed us under. Regardless of the category of sickness, deliverance can come only from God, but it is only bestowed upon those who truly want deliverance. Some people prefer to dwell in their infirmities. They cry out to God in their misery, but they wouldn't give up their misery for anything. They are self-righteous and lovers of self.

We should want to escape our heartaches and afflictions when we realize the spiritual effects they have on us. Anything that causes physical, mental and financial problems will eventually have a spiritual effect as well. All of these phases of sickness can hinder our relationship with God. Those who are sincere in righteousness will cry out to God for help.

In our Scripture text, David proclaims the effects of crying out to God. He says, *"The righteous* cry, and the LORD heareth, and delivereth them out of all their troubles." These troubles he refers to are sicknesses, strongholds and even daily struggles. God is faithful to deliver the righteous.

The text goes on to reveal what it takes to receive deliverance. Verse 18 says, "The LORD *is* nigh unto them that are of a broken heart; and saveth such as be of a contrite spirit." Deliverance comes to one whose heart is broken and whose spirit is contrite. We must get to the point where we acknowledge that God is our only hope, and then we can be delivered. Strongholds will be lifted from us and liberty in the Lord prevails.

We can be healed because of who we are in Christ Jesus. It doesn't matter if your affliction is of the heart, the mind or the flesh. God's Word says, "Many *are* the afflictions of the righteous: but the LORD delivereth him out of them all." We can't receive this truth because we refuse to accept God's definition of healing.

Sin sickness was healed at Calvary through the shed blood of Jesus Christ. We may still live under the effects of sin's strongholds, but sin cannot destroy us. First John 1:9 says, "If we confess our sins, he is faithful and just to forgive us *our* sins, and to cleanse us from all unrighteousness." That's the remedy for sin sickness. Start confessing your sin, and watch God start delivering.

Mind battles are another type of sickness. They create more ailments such as fear, stress, worry and doubt. These ailments eventually lead us into sin because we allow them to control our relationship with God. The remedy for this sickness is found in Romans 12:2: "And be not conformed to this world: but be ye transformed by the renewing of your mind, that ye may prove what *is* that good, and acceptable, and perfect, will of God." To overcome the battles of the mind, you must transform your thoughts to conform to the Word of God.

Spiritual sickness is the sickness of broken fellowship with God. It also refers to those times when, even though we know we're saved, we can't seem to see or hear God. This sickness is brought on by sin, mind battles and the enemy. Satan wants you to feel distant and abandoned by God. If he can convince you that God has abandoned you, then he can control your mind and bring about physical ailments and sin in your body. The remedy for this sickness is found in Hebrews 13:5: "*Let your* conversation *be* without covetousness; *and be* content with such things as ye have: for he hath said, I will never leave thee, nor forsake thee." An additional remedy is found in James 4:7-8: "Submit yourselves therefore to God. Resist the devil, and he will flee from you. [8]Draw nigh to God, and he will draw nigh to you. Cleanse *your* hands, *ye* sinners; and purify *your* hearts, *ye* double minded." Spiritual sickness does not have to be present in our lives. Jesus died so that you could have life more abundant.

"Spiritual sickness is the sickness of broken fellowship with God."

Physical sickness is probably the most misunderstood in God's Word. Many people battle with why some people are healed physically while others are not. Sometimes, God's grace is sufficient. Paul was not healed of his thorn in the flesh, but God promised that His grace would see Paul through it. God also told Paul that he would be made strong in his weakness (2 Corinthians 12:8-10).

God may not choose to heal you physically, but He will give you grace to endure. Often, our physical sickness gets better as our dependence upon God gets greater and we become more mentally and spiritually stable. Then, we begin to deal with our physical ailments with hope in God. Physical sickness is something we will all deal with in this life. It is a fact of life, and we must learn to depend upon God for strength to endure.

Again, Psalm 37:19 says, "Many *are* the afflictions of the righteous: but the LORD delivereth him out of them all."

How often do you cry out to the Lord in your afflictions? _____
_____

Are you allowing God to transform your mind?_____
_____

In our Scripture text, how does God say we must come to Him?_____
_____

Based on this week's study, on which process of healing do you need to focus? Circle your answer:

Determination   Discipline   Dependence   Defense   Deliverance

Daily Reflections: Your Thoughts on Today's Study

_____

_____

_____

_____

_____

_____

_____

_____

Prayer Journal: Your Prayer on Today's Study

_____

_____

_____

_____

_____

_____

_____

Chapter 9

The Unveiling

Romans 12:1: *"I beseech you therefore, brethren, by the mercies of God, that ye present your bodies a living sacrifice, holy, acceptable unto God, which is your reasonable service."*

For the past eight weeks, we have examined ourselves and found our flaws. We have covered the processes which change the way we think, the way we live and our whole outlook on life. Some of these things we changed or applied immediately. Others took some time to comprehend. Perhaps you haven't completely comprehended it yet, but the principles are working to make you new inside.

We have taken a long, hard look in the mirror. We've faced the facts, dealt with reality, transformed our minds, revived our hearts, and nursed our wounds. We've learned how to overcome the pain as we allow the healing process to begin. Friends, we have experienced an extreme makeover. Some weeks of the makeover have been more rewarding than others, but all have been beneficial to us for spiritual growth.

"The changes God wants us to reveal are those He has made from within."

If you've been receptive to each phase of the transformation, then you are ready to reveal the results of your makeover. You should have an excitement about the changes your makeover has produced. Remember, some of the surface and hidden things may not be completely healed yet, but the extreme differences in you will outshine those unhealed areas until they are better.

Our Scripture text urges us to unveil the only transformation that will be eternally effective. It states that we are to present our bodies a living sacrifice, holy, acceptable unto God. This is our reasonable service. Any other type of transformation will only be a temporary satisfaction of the flesh.

The changes God wants us to reveal are those He has made from within. The outward changes that we make cannot point others to Jesus Christ. Unveiling the makeover of the inward man reveals the transforming power of God. This is our reasonable service.

When people see changes taking place in our lives, they should see:

- Refreshing
- Righteousness
- Restoration
- Reconciliation
- Radiance

Day 1   *Refreshing*

Acts 3:19: *"Repent ye therefore, and be converted, that your sins may be blotted out, when the times of refreshing shall come from the presence of the Lord."*

Absolutely nothing is more refreshing than being in the presence of the Lord. The quickest way to put ourselves in heavenly places is to repent; we must turn to God. Repent has a double meaning. It can mean to turn from something or to turn to something.

Turning to God brings refreshing. It converts our ways and our lifestyles and transforms our minds. Turning to God blots out our sins, and cleanses our hearts from evil. It brings about righteousness in our lives.

Refreshing comes as we allow our lives to be transformed by the truth and holiness of God. The Bible teaches that the truth will make us free, and as we become free we become refreshed. We look, act, think, walk and talk differently when we live in truth. Our frowns turn to smiles, our distress turns to joy, and our confusion turns to peace.

Everyone will notice the changes as God makes us over from the inside out. Refreshing will be evident in every area of your relationship with God. We are drawn into His presence as we allow Him to transform our lives. The more we sup with Him, the more like Him we become.

I remember when a particular time of refreshing came in my own life. Everyone around me watched as God totally transformed my life. As God unveiled the changes, everyone saw the new work that God was doing. I didn't have to say anything to them; the change was obvious. I went from being depressed and suicidal to being joyous and full of life. I was transformed from a life of negative speaking and thinking to a life of positivity. I started finding good in every bad situation. I found myself praying and praising God even when everything looked hopeless. I was refreshed in the Lord. The inward change was so drastic that it became outwardly effective, too. My speech changed; my countenance lifted; even my body language improved. I started feeling loved. I learned to love myself, and I started loving others with God's love. I felt like a new person. In fact, I had become new through the transforming truth of God's Word. That change took place over 15 years ago, and still today I feel refreshed in the Lord.

When days of heartache and pain come, we must get in the presence of the Lord to renew our refreshing. We have been made new in Christ, and nothing can separate us from His love. Romans 8:35-39 confirms this for us:

Who shall separate us from the love of Christ? *shall* tribulation, or distress, or persecution, or famine, or nakedness, or peril, or sword? [36]As it is written, For thy sake we are killed all the day long; we are accounted as sheep for the slaughter. [37]Nay, in all these things we are more than conquerors through him that loved us. [38]For I am persuaded, that neither death, nor life, nor angels, nor principalities, nor powers, nor things present, nor things to come, [39]Nor height, nor depth, nor any other creature, shall be able to separate us from the love of God, which is in Christ Jesus our Lord.

We find our refreshing in the blessed truth of this Scripture. As a child of God, you can live both refreshed and unveiled in His presence.

Do others see the refreshing of the Lord upon you? _____
_____

Are there sins in your life from which you need to be converted? If so, what are they?_____
_____
_____

What does repent mean? _____
_____

How has your life changed since you received the Lord as your Savior?_____
_____

Record a time of refreshing in your life. Record the change God made in you and the circumstances surrounding the refreshing. _____
_____
_____
_____
_____
_____
_____

Daily Reflections: *Your Thoughts on Today's Study*

_____

_____

_____

_____

_____

_____

_____

_____

_____

Prayer Journal: *Your Prayer on Today's Study*

_____

_____

_____

_____

_____

_____

_____

Day 2 *Righteousness*

1 Peter 2:24: *"Who his own self bare our sins in his own body on the tree, that we, being dead to sins, should live unto righteousness: by whose stripes ye were healed."*

Your life was transformed from sin to righteousness in Christ when you were born again (saved). Jesus hung on a tree, bearing our sin so that we could live in righteousness. Our Scripture text says that we are healed by His stripes.

At Calvary, Jesus underwent a transformation from sinless and holiness to being cursed on a tree as He became sin for you and me. Galatians 3:13 says, "Christ hath redeemed us from the curse of the law, being made a curse for us: for it is written, Cursed *is* every one that hangeth on a tree." The perfect, holy, sinless One became sin, and because God cannot look upon sin, He turned His back on His only begotten Son. By Jesus' stripes, our sin sickness was healed. On an old, rugged cross, He made a way for you and me to live a life of righteousness.

Righteousness was imputed to us when we received Christ as our personal Savior. It is unveiled as we live in the holiness of Jesus Christ. As we surrender to His will, we become examples of righteousness for all to see.

The desires we once had for the world and sin begin to vanish when we receive Christ. A new desire to live righteously and pleasing to God becomes evident in all we do. A life of righteousness speaks volumes of peace and joy to those who are watching us.

The transformation God is doing in your life will make you the center of attention. All eyes are on you! Your transformation of righteousness will be tried and tested by both your peers and your enemies. Satan seeks to destroy the changes God is making in you.

Your responsibility is to maintain the transformation that God has done in your life. You were not transformed for your glory, but for the glory of God. Maintaining this transformation will require work and sacrifice on your part. You will have to:

- Bathe yourself in the Word of God (Ephesians 5:26-27).
- Cleanse your mind with Truth (1 Samuel 12:24).
- Clothe yourself with the whole armor of God (Ephesians 6:13-18).
- Walk in the light (1 John 1:7-8).
- Talk with boldness (1 John 4:17).
- Stand against the wiles of the devil (Ephesians 6:11).
- Live as a peculiar person (1 Peter 2:9).

As you demonstrate the righteous work that God has performed in and through you, people will be watching. They will be amazed at how beautiful and radiant you are in the Lord. The inner work that God has done in you will resonate into the lives of those surrounding you. Your righteousness will penetrate the lives of hurting, hopeless people, and God will be pleased with you.

We must remember that righteousness is not to be harbored and kept secret. God intends for all who are righteous and sincere to share the great work He has done in them with others. We should never be ashamed of what God has done in our lives. Romans 1:16-18 says, "For I am not ashamed of the gospel of Christ: for it is the power of God unto salvation to every one that believeth; to the Jew first, and also to the Greek. [17]For therein is the righteousness of God revealed from faith to faith: as it is written, The just shall live by faith. [18]For the wrath of God is revealed from heaven against all ungodliness and unrighteousness of men, who hold the truth in unrighteousness"

"Righteousness is not to be harbored and kept secret."

God has made you over. Your life should demonstrate righteousness. Allow God to unveil His great work through you.

Are you harboring or demonstrating the righteousness of God? _____

_____

Have you or are you unveiling these characteristics of righteousness in the lives of others?

Love   Respect   Forgiveness   Trust   Kindness

Truth   Humility   Joy

How have your desires changed since God did a makeover on you? _____

_____

Daily Reflections: Your Thoughts on Today's Study

_____

_____

_____

_____

_____

_____

_____

_____

Prayer Journal: Your Prayer on Today's Study

_____

_____

_____

_____

_____

_____

_____

Day 3   *Restoration*

Psalm 51:10-12: *"Create in me a clean heart, O God; and renew a right spirit within me. [11]Cast me not away from thy presence; and take not thy holy spirit from me. [12]Restore unto me the joy of thy salvation; and uphold me with thy free spirit."*

Restoration is the product of complete healing. When our lives have been transformed by the power of God, everything that was once painful and devastating seems to disappear. The joy of our salvation is restored through Jesus Christ.

Restoration can be an unpleasant process, because pain is often experienced during the healing of a wound. The Scriptures teach that the Bible is a two-edged sword. It cuts out the old nature while cleansing and restoring our lives to love and health. As restoration takes place, the transformation is revealed.

Restoration makes us more energetic, more positive, more motivated and more in love with Jesus. Restoration is usually thought to be for the body and mind, but our souls also need to be restored. The body and the mind can not survive without spiritual restoration.

"Restoration makes us more energetic, more positive, more motivated and more in love with Jesus."

Regardless of how intimate your relationship with God is, issues will arise that the enemy will use as a setback in your life. These things usually come up unexpectedly. We've studied Naomi previously. Her setback was the death of her husband and sons. Her grief seemed to be more than she could handle, but her restoration came through Ruth and Boaz. Ruth 4:14-15 says, "And the women said unto Naomi, Blessed *be* the LORD, which hath not left thee this day without a kinsman, that his name may be famous in Israel. [15]And he shall be unto thee a restorer of *thy* life, and a nourisher of thine old age: for thy daughter in law, which loveth thee, which is better to thee than seven sons, hath born him."

Joseph's setback was the betrayal he suffered at the hands of his brothers. His restoration also came from this betrayal, because he was promoted from the slavery his brothers sold him into to being second in command of Egypt where he ruled over his brothers.

The longings of the flesh caused David's setback. He allowed his desire for Bathsheba to override the righteousness of God in his life. David's restoration was painful; it cost him the life of his son. Still, he was restored.

We will face unexpected setbacks, and we will be wounded by them. Satan wants to destroy the healing of God that has taken place in your life, but God's makeover plan is designed to last for eternity. We must simply trust in Him to maintain the makeover. Naomi's joy was made new. Joseph's family was restored, and he earned the respect of others. David's joy in the Lord was restored, and the man after God's own heart was spiritually made over.

What was made over in the lives of all of these people? Their zeal for God was restored. They became motivated in righteousness, and they became examples of God's goodness. Your life is allowed setbacks for the same purpose. Restoration is appreciated so much more when the wounded victim has experienced great conflict.

Our Scripture text reveals that David's setback prepared his heart for a spiritual cleansing and divine restoration. David cried, "Create in me a clean heart, O God." Then, "Restore unto me the joy of thy salvation."

Restoration produces:

- A clean heart.
- A ready heart.
- A joyous heart.
- A thankful heart.
- A servant's heart.

In which of these areas does your heart need restoration? Underline the answer above.

God is working to restore your joy as well as your love, compassion, trust and motivation. Allow Him to heal you completely so that you, too, can unveil the restoration Jesus Christ has performed in your life.

Which of these elements of spiritual restoration are you lacking? Circle your answer(s) below.

Motivation   Energy   Faith   Trust   Joy   Peace   Other

Which Biblical example best describes your most recent setback?

- ☐ Naomi, angry and bitter
- ☐ Joseph, hurt and betrayed
- ☐ David, lustful and deceptive

Daily Reflections: Your Thoughts on Today's Study

_____

_____

_____

_____

_____

_____

_____

_____

Prayer Journal: Your Prayer on Today's Study

_____

_____

_____

_____

_____

_____

_____

Day 4   *Reconciliation*

2 Corinthians 5:18: *"And all things are of God, who hath reconciled us to himself by Jesus Christ, and hath given to us the ministry of reconciliation."*

Each phase of our transformation is another step in the right direction. We grow closer and closer to God as we allow Him to unveil His power and presence within us. We who have received Jesus as our Savior have become joint heirs with Him through His crucifixion, the shedding of His blood and His resurrection. We have been reconciled to God through the work of Calvary.

Reconciliation implies being brought back into fellowship with God. Our Scripture text says, "God, who hath reconciled us to himself by Jesus Christ." Now, He has given us the ministry of reconciliation. If we have been reconciled to God through Jesus, then we have the power to help reconcile others to Him as well. Our focus should be on serving others and teaching them the principles of being one with Christ.

Our lives have been changed from the inside out. We are to live out that change with boldness and confidence. We should act like children of the King; that is who we are. That doesn't mean we should be boastful and haughty; it means we should be dependent and dedicated to God wherever we go and in whatever we do.

The Bible says that as joint heirs with Jesus we should:

- Be holy as He is holy.
- Walk in the light as He is in the light.
- Love the brethren.
- Be doers of the word and not hearers only.

If we are truly reconciled (in full fellowship) with God, these are our basic responsibilities as part of the family of God. These things will be noticed by others, but it is our responsibility to unveil them to others.

It can be difficult to tell if someone has been reconciled to God. Their mouth may speak it, but their actions fail to demonstrate it. If there's been a makeover, it can't be seen by others. If we don't demonstrate what we speak, then our walk and our talk hinder the work of God for our lives.

True reconciliation speaks volumes just through our actions. Words are not necessary when our actions are in line with the Word of God. Acts 11:26 says, "And the disciples were called Christians first in Antioch." They will call you a Christian, too, if your actions speak louder than your words about the transforming power of Christ.

Are you living as if you have been reconciled to God?_____

Are you living a ministry of reconciliation? _____

_____

Who has been your latest challenge of reconciliation?_____

_____

Daily Reflections: Your Thoughts on Today's Study

_____

_____

_____

_____

_____

_____

_____

_____

Prayer Journal: *Your Prayer on Today's Study*

_____

_____

_____

_____

_____

_____

_____

Day 5   *Radiance*

Proverbs 4:18: *"But the path of the just is as the shining light, that shineth more and more unto the perfect day."*

This week we have allowed God to unveil the transformation He has made in our lives. We have stood refreshed, spoken righteousness, exemplified restoration, demonstrated reconciliation; now it's time to just radiate the love of Jesus for the great work He has done.

The Great Physician is the light shining more and more unto the perfect day in our lives. He longs to shine through you. You are His vessel, the tool of righteousness He uses to reconcile others to Himself.

Our greatest desire should be to be that shining light that radiates the mercy and grace of our Lord and Savior. It is one thing to profess Christianity, but it is quite another to radiate through our thoughts and actions. Basically, our Scripture text says that God will shine more and more through us if we'll only allow Him to do so.

"Your transformation to radiance began at salvation."

Have you ever known someone with severe acne or other potentially disfiguring ailments? Once, a lady was plagued with a skin disease that had attacked her face. It caused her skin to be scaly, and she felt ugly. She became discouraged and depressed because of her low self-esteem. She battled this disease for years before she finally found a physician who offered her a cure. He knew the procedure to both remove the scales and restore her natural radiance and beauty. She went through a very long and painful healing process. It worked, and now she is a beautiful woman. She radiates joy and confidence. She can laugh again, and she holds her head high when she walks through a crowd. What brought about this change in her? She allowed the doctor to do what he thought would work for her, and he transformed her into a radiant beauty.

When we allow God to work through our lives in the way He sees best, the presence of the Lord will radiate from our heart into the lives of others. We, too, can walk through crowds with our heads held high. We can laugh again because we live in the confidence of God Almighty. We can have an unshakable confidence in our relationship with Him. Even our darkest days can radiate the light of His presence if we'll just allow Him to shine through us. Do you trust Him to perform the right procedure to bring out His beauty in you?

Your transformation to radiance began at salvation. God is working in your life daily to shine through you more and more. Romans 12:1 says, "I beseech you therefore, brethren, by the mercies of God, that ye present your bodies a living sacrifice, holy, acceptable unto God, *which is* your reasonable service."

How confident are you in the Lord? _____

_____

Are you radiating the power of Jesus?_____

_____

Are you allowing Him to light your path?_____

_____

Daily Reflections: Your Thoughts on Today's Study

_____

_____

_____

_____

_____

_____

_____

_____

Prayer Journal: *Your Prayer on Today's Study*

_____

_____

_____

_____

_____

_____

Chapter 10

Made Over

2 Corinthians 5:17: *"Therefore if any man be in Christ, he is a new creature: old things are passed away; behold, all things are become new."*

Well, my friends, we have come to the end of our makeover. The title of our study should be coming to life for you by now. If your heart has been sincere toward God during this endeavor, you should be well on your way to a total transformation.

It may have been a long, painful journey, but you can rejoice in that you are now a new creature. In Christ Jesus, your old life has passed away and all things are made new. Only Jesus has the power to make that happen, and He did it in you!

When you were born again, you became the dwelling place for the Holy Spirit of God. He now lives in and through you. When you received Jesus, you also received a new name in glory. When Abram was made over, he became Abraham. When God did a makeover on Sarai, she became Sarah. Jacob's makeover transformed his name to Israel, and Saul became Paul. Salvation by grace through faith makes us brand new in every aspect of the word.

"As children of God, we will never again be who we used to be."

Being made new sets us at liberty with the Lord. We now have access to the throne room where we can make our requests known unto God. We actually became royalty, and that's exactly how the Savior sees us. We are children of the King. When God sees us, He sees the royal blood that was shed for us. Ephesians 1:6-7 says, "To the praise of the glory of his grace, wherein he hath made us accepted in the beloved. [7]In whom we have redemption through his blood, the forgiveness of sins, according to the riches of his grace."

We are accepted in the beloved through Christ's work on Calvary. We were not simply remodeled. We were made new; we became a new work. His precious blood did not renovate what was in our lives. He did away with the old stuff. Our Scripture text says that the old is passed away. We are new creatures in Christ Jesus!

As children of God, we will never again be who we used to be. We're no longer those people. The work God has done in our lives has buried the past. Our present life He carries, and our future's so much brighter because our lives have been made over. We do not belong here in this present world; we are only passing through. We do not fit into this world's system because of who we are in Christ. We should have no desire to fit in here. Instead, we should long to be more like Him every day.

Our vision for life should be changing. We don't have to struggle to be accepted; we can be happy with who we are. We don't have to fight to keep up with the world and its requirements. We have a new perspective on life since we've been made over. We've completed the transformation from a lowly caterpillar to a splendid butterfly. We can't go back to the cocoon; it's gone. We've been made over from one extreme to another.

The Potter has taken a simple lump of clay and made the masterpiece that only He could foresee. He knew our potential before He ever placed us on His wheel. With His precious hands, He molded and made us into vessels to be used for His honor and glory.

The Potter works each piece of clay with skill and vision. He gently removes the impurities that can weaken the final work while scribing His perfect plan into each piece. I wrote the following poem to help define the analogy of our lives being made over like a piece of clay on the potter's wheel:

The Potter's Hand

With His hands He works the clay
Upon the Potter's wheel.
He gently forms the pattern
With purpose and with skill.
With steady, careful shaping
His vessel is created,
Fired, glazed and colored,
Then beautifully decorated.
Just a worthless piece of clay
Has been fashioned with finesse.
The Potter made each piece
Exquisite and priceless.

Our relationship with God can be looked at through the analogy of the Potter and the clay or the analogy of the Physician and the patient. The Potter makes us what He knows we can be, and the Great Physician can do in our lives the things man says cannot be done.

Our lives have been fashioned by both the Potter and the Physician. God is at work in our lives in both ways each day. The Potter is continuously placing us on His wheel, working out our impurities. Meanwhile, the Physician is removing the diseases of sin, bad habits and rebellion.

As we study how our lives are made new in Christ Jesus, we will focus on the analogy of the Potter. We are the clay in His hands. As we go through the process of becoming a useful vessel, our lives will be:

- Molded
- Shaped
- Glazed
- Fired
- Displayed

Day 1   *Molded*

Philippians 3:21: *"Who shall change our vile body, that it may be fashioned like unto his glorious body, according to the working whereby he is able even to subdue all things unto himself."*

Our lives were made over the moment we were saved. The work Jesus did at Calvary is fashioning us into His likeness. Day by day, we are being made into His image, and when we finally reach our heavenly home, even our bodies will be made like unto His according to our Scripture text.

As He molds the clay of our lives, we should begin to live more Christ-like. We take more and more of the shape of the mold as we seek Him, talk to Him, strive to please Him and long to be more like Him daily.

Think about it like this: Jesus is holy. When you received Him, you became holy. Holiness is part of His mold. Jesus is righteousness; when you received Him, you received His righteousness. Righteousness is also a part of His mold. This is what our Scripture text refers to when it says that He changes our vile bodies like unto His glorious body.

What does it take to be molded?

- Place yourself in the Potter's hands.
- Allow Him to mold you into His image.
- Let go of the impurities in your life.
- Learn as much as you can about Jesus.
- Strive to do what Jesus would do.
- Study the personality of God.
- Apply all that you learn about God to your own life.

If you follow these guidelines, you will find yourself tightly fitting into the Savior's mold of holiness and humility.

List one area of your life that has been made more Christ-like in your makeover._____

_____

How long did it take for this area of your life to be molded into His image? __

_____

_____

List one area of your life that still needs to be fashioned according to His mold. _____

_____

Daily Reflections: *Your Thoughts on Today's Study*

_____

_____

_____

_____

_____

_____

_____

_____

_____

Prayer Journal: *Your Prayer on Today's Study*

_____

_____

_____

_____

_____

_____

_____

Day 2   *Shaping*

Jeremiah 18:4: *"And the vessel that he made of clay was marred in the hand of the potter: so he made it again another vessel, as seemed good to the potter to make it."*

Your life has already been made new through salvation, but God continues to work the clay because we are never plucked from His hands. If we become marred in some way, He makes us again into another vessel. God can and will shape our lives into whatever He needs them to be.

Esther's life was shaped into a vessel of deliverance for a whole nation of people. God shaped her in faith, beauty, boldness and courage to save the Jews from certain death. God knew Esther's heart. He placed her before the King in all her beauty so that she could be a vessel for His glory.

God saved you for a purpose. He wants to shape you into an effective vessel that can be used to further His kingdom work. Your life was made over for righteousness' sake, and you will be held accountable for how you use your new life in Him. As vessels of the master Potter, we should desire to be fashioned into His image.

"God will shape, shape and reshape us until we adhere to His mold."

Our Scripture text says, "The vessel that he made of clay was marred in the hand of the potter." What does this imply? The original Hebrew word for marred means to be destroyed or crushed. The reason for this crushing is explained in the remainder of the verse: "So he made it again another vessel, as seemed good to the potter to make *it.*"

God will shape, shape and reshape us until we adhere to His mold. He knows the plans He has for us, and He intends for His plans to be fulfilled. One small impurity or weak area can put us back on the Potter's wheel to be reshaped. God will make another vessel that is stronger, purer and more useful.

Self-will causes us to need reshaping. We often work against the hand of the Potter, causing weak points and flaws in the Potter's piece of art. We leave Him no other option than to crush us and put us back on the wheel.

The Potter has all authority over the piece of clay. He can do with us as He chooses: crush us, destroy us, even put us up on a shelf. His desire is to shape your life into something that He can use and display for all the world to see.

God uses all shapes and sizes of clay in His kingdom work. He uses weak vessels, shallow vessels, strong vessels and deep vessels. He places each piece where He knows it will be most effective, and then He becomes the strength of the vessel. We do not have to worry over our ability to be used for God's work; He can take the weakest vessel and make it strong.

As God's vessel, what shape are you? Perhaps you feel weak and fragile, at the point of collapsing. The Potter's hand is upon you. He is protecting you from destruction and defeat. Allow Him to reshape and strengthen you for the purpose He created you to fulfill.

Remember, Esther did not feel like she could be used. Her past and family background made her feel useless and ineffective, but God chose her for His work. He placed her before the king, and He used her in the palace for His good and His glory.

God is also shaping you into His perfect will. He sees your potential. He wants to shape you into the image of His Son. He is working these things into your life to make you more like Him:

- Love
- Peace
- Joy
- Forgiveness
- Gentleness
- Humility
- Servanthood
- Self-denial
- Self-sacrifice

The list could go on and on, but you get the point.

Which of these things do you need the Potter to work into your life? _____
_____

List the things in your life that you feel need to be crushed and worked into a new vessel in the Potter's hands._____
_____
_____

Are you faithful enough to the Potter to surrender this to Him? _____
_____

Daily Reflections: Your Thoughts on Today's Study

_____

_____

_____

_____

_____

_____

_____

_____

Prayer Journal: Your Prayer on Today's Study

_____

_____

_____

_____

_____

_____

_____

Day 3   *Glazed*

Revelation 19:8: *"And to her was granted that she should be arrayed in fine linen, clean and white: for the fine linen is the righteousness of saints."*

The World Book Encyclopedia states that glazing a piece of clay or pottery is done not only to decorate it, but also to smooth and waterproof it. After it is glazed, the pottery is fired. We will study the firing process tomorrow.

We were sealed with the Holy Spirit of promise when Jesus came into our hearts. Like glazing the pottery makes it resistant to water, the Spirit dart-proofed our lives. We are now resistant to the fiery darts of the devil. Jesus smoothed us out with the anointing power of the Holy Spirit, and He decorated our lives with His righteousness.

According to our Scripture text, we can walk in the power of righteousness. We have been granted to be arrayed in fine linen, clean and white through the precious blood of the Lamb. His blood is the glazing upon our lives. It was applied at salvation, and it has cleansed us whiter than snow. We have a gloss about us that the lost do not have. Jesus shines in our lives. We are vessels adorned for His service.

"God's desire is not that you should sit on a shelf collecting dust."

God gave us this shiny glaze of radiance to draw the attention of those whose lives are dulled by the effects of sin and unrighteousness. This is not for our glory, but for His. The attention drawn by the glow of our glaze should be directed to God alone. This life is not about us; it's all about Him.

The glazing process also involves a design. Each piece created by God is original and unique. Isaiah 43:21 says, "This people have I formed for myself; they shall show forth my praise."

My friend, you have been glazed or arrayed in the fine linen which is the righteousness of the saints. You are to show forth the work which the Potter has performed in your life. God's desire is not that you should sit on a shelf collecting dust. He sealed you with His Holy Spirit, and He expects you to show forth the joy of His redeeming love.

As God's design of righteousness, where do you feel most effective in His service? _____

_____

Have there been times when you felt you were just sitting on a shelf? If so, describe your experience here. _____

_____

_____

_____

Do you feel that you now represent the righteousness of saints to others? If not, why? _____

_____

_____

_____

Daily Reflections: *Your Thoughts on Today's Study*

_____

_____

_____

_____

_____

_____

_____

Prayer Journal: *Your Prayer on Today's Study*

_____

_____

_____

_____

_____

_____

Day 4   *Fired*

1 Peter 1:7: *"That the trial of your faith, being much more precious than of gold that perisheth, though it be tried with fire, might be found unto praise and honour and glory at the appearing of Jesus Christ."*

Regardless of our strength as a Christian, there will be times in our journey when our faith is tried. God allows us to be put through the fire so that we become purer and stronger soldiers of Christ.

When the pottery is fired, it is placed into an oven or kiln set to a very high temperature. The heat makes the potter strong and durable. It also makes the glaze stick to the clay, and it hardens the glaze as well. If the piece is not placed in the fire, it will not be able to withstand pressure. The enemy can detect our weaknesses, and his goal is to make sure you are not strengthened for the battle.

"Going through the fire is a difficult task, but in the end you will be found faithful and pleasing to God."

Going through the fire is a difficult task, but in the end you will be found faithful and pleasing to God. Second Timothy 4:5 says, "But watch thou in all things, endure afflictions, do the work of an evangelist, make full proof of thy ministry." The firing process requires us to endure the heat of the flames. In Scripture, fire is figurative of the power and presence of the Holy Spirit, and it symbolizes purification.

Isaiah's commission from God involved purification through a live coal in the hand of the seraphim. Isaiah 6:5-9 says:

> Then said I, Woe *is* me! for I am undone; because I *am* a man of unclean lips, and I dwell in the midst of a people of unclean lips: for mine eyes have seen the King, the LORD of hosts. [6]Then flew one of the seraphims unto me, having a live coal in his hand, *which* he had taken with the tongs from off the altar: [7]And he laid *it* upon my mouth, and said, Lo, this hath touched thy lips; and thine iniquity is taken away, and thy sin purged. [8]Also I heard the voice of the Lord, saying, Whom shall I send, and who will go for us? Then said I, Here *am* I; send me.

Isaiah willingly went through this purification process. He was purged from his sin and iniquity, and he came forth as gold when he was tried with the hot coal to his lips. God had a molded, shaped, glazed and fired vessel in Isaiah. God would use him for His purpose, because Isaiah wanted to be used.

God prepared his heart for the service ahead, and this man of God became meet for the Master's use.

God did a new thing in Isaiah's life. The fire strengthened and prepared Isaiah to go wherever God might send him. It removed all the impurities that might have held back this chosen man of God. This live coal firing was a part of Isaiah's commission.

When God calls and commissions us for service, we can expect to be tried by fire. Under pressure, we will either collapse or harden. God's plan is for us to be strong and sturdy vessels of honor.

God loves you, and He will not leave you to go through the firing process alone. He will be there with you. When Shadrach, Meshech and Abednego were thrown into the fiery furnace, God was right there with them. He did a new thing in the lives of those three men. We find several principles of the firing process through Isaiah and the three men in the fiery furnace. The firing process:

- Purges sin.
- Purifies hearts.
- Prepares for service.

We have no need to fear the fire. God is preparing to use you for His kingdom, and He has promised that we will come forth as gold. You will not perish under the pressure as long as you place your faith in God. The firing process is not to prove your strength to God; its purpose is to show you your own strengths and weaknesses. God already knows if you will be able to withstand the test. The firing process is for your benefit.

When God saved you, you were given power to fight, overcome and succeed against every adversary that might come against you. The battles are meant to teach you, to increase your faith and to make you a stronger Christian. To achieve these things as you go through the fire, you must:

- Put on the armor of God (it's fireproof).
- Walk by faith (sight will mislead you).
- Trust in God (not in man).
- Expect deliverance (defeat belongs to Satan).

Everything you do for God will be tried by fire. Make sure that your heart is sincere and your commission is fulfilled. God is an all-knowing God, and He will test your works. He made you new and shaped your life to serve Him. First Corinthians 3:13 says, "Every man's work shall be made manifest: for the day shall declare it, because it shall be revealed by fire; and the fire shall try every man's work of what sort it is."

Like Isaiah, are you willing to be fired? _____

Have you been put through the fire lately? If so, record the circumstances and experience of your trial here._____

_____

How did you come through your trial by fire:

☐ Stronger
☐ Collapsed
☐ Defeated

Which part of the pottery process do you most feel you need to experience?

☐ Molding
☐ Shaping
☐ Glazing
☐ Firing

Daily Reflections: *Your Thoughts on Today's Study*

_____

_____

_____

_____

_____

_____

_____

_____

_____

Prayer Journal: *Your Prayer on Today's Study*

_____

_____

_____

_____

_____

_____

_____

Day 5   *Displayed*

Psalm 60:4: *"Thou hast given a banner to them that fear thee, that it may be displayed because of the truth."*

Here, my friend, in our Scripture text is the whole purpose for being made over from the inside out. The truth of God must be displayed in our lives. Truth is the banner which God expects us to wave. God created us to uphold a standard of godliness that should supercede anything else in our lives.

We were placed here on this earth to manifest the glorious Gospel of Jesus Christ. God formed us in our mothers' wombs so that we could be disciples of the Word of God. Our love for God should build a reverence for Him that is demonstrated in everyday life.

Each morning as we start our day, we should look in the mirror and thank God for the makeover He has performed in our hearts and lives. If for some reason you have lost sight of what He has done for you, then you need to reflect back on the past and realize that you are alive and blessed today because of God's love, grace and mercy.

"Truth is the foundation of who you are."

Truth is the foundation of who you are, not only as a Christian but also as a parent, companion, co-worker and friend. Relationships should be built on truth. Your witness as a Christian should demonstrate truth and sincerity. John 3:21 says, "But he that doeth truth cometh to the light, that his deeds may be made manifest, that they are wrought in God." Each time we speak truth, we guard ourselves with the power of God.

The Word of God is truth. It is the only thing that will neither deceive us nor let us down. If we guard our hearts and minds by absorbing God's Word, then our inward change will transform our outward appearance. When we live in truth, we live unto Jesus Christ. John 1:17 says, "For the law was given by Moses, *but* grace and truth came by Jesus Christ."

The power of truth is demonstrated when we live by its five principles (which were originally preached by my husband, Dan Robinson):

- Truth. It makes us free. John 8:31-32 says, "Then said Jesus to those Jews which believed on him, If ye continue in my word, *then* are ye my disciples indeed; [32]And ye shall know the truth, and the truth shall make you free."
- Relationship. Truth puts us into an intimate relationship with God. John 15:1-5 says, "I am the true vine, and my Father is the husband-

man. [2]Every branch in me that beareth not fruit he taketh away: and every *branch* that beareth fruit, he purgeth it, that it may bring forth more fruit. [3]Now ye are clean through the word which I have spoken unto you. [4]Abide in me, and I in you. As the branch cannot bear fruit of itself, except it abide in the vine; no more can ye, except ye abide in me. [5]I am the vine, ye *are* the branches: He that abideth in me, and I in him, the same bringeth forth much fruit: for without me ye can do nothing."

- Unity. Truth draws us into unity with God and others. Ephesians 4:13-15: "Till we all come in the unity of the faith, and of the knowledge of the Son of God, unto a perfect man, unto the measure of the stature of the fulness of Christ: [14]That we *henceforth* be no more children, tossed to and fro, and carried about with every wind of doctrine, by the sleight of men, *and* cunning craftiness, whereby they lie in wait to deceive."

- Trust. As we trust God, we realize He cannot and will not lie, deceive us or let us down. Isaiah 26:3-4: "Thou wilt keep *him* in perfect peace, *whose* mind *is* stayed *on thee*: because he trusteth in thee. [4]Trust ye in the LORD for ever: for in the LORD JEHOVAH *is* everlasting strength."

- Hope. God is truth, and in Him we have hope. First John 3:2-3 says, "Beloved, now are we the sons of God, and it doth not yet appear what we shall be: but we know that, when he shall appear, we shall be like him; for we shall see him as he is. [3]And every man that hath this hope in him purifieth himself, even as he is pure."

Truth resides in you, and His name is Jesus. He demonstrates His person through your life as you adhere to His precepts.

I pray that you will continue to look in the mirror and review your relationship with God. The truest mirror is God's Word. It will reveal the changes you have already made and the ones you still need to make. God will guide you through every transformation, and He will perfect everything about you until you look, act, walk and talk just like Jesus. Romans 8:29 says, "For whom he did foreknow, he also did predestinate *to be* conformed to the image of his Son, that he might be the firstborn among many brethren."

The Potter is conforming you to the image of His Son. Your life is a display of God's wondrous works, an affirmation of His faithfulness and creation. This song goes perfectly with this subject and should certainly be our closing song of victory.

Made Over

My life has been made over, from one extreme to another.
From a life of sin to righteousness in Him
Through the precious blood of the Lamb
My life has been made over.
When I look at where I come from to the life that I now live
I know that God has done a work according to His will
My past is now buried, my present life He carries
My future's so much brighter because
My life has been made over, from one extreme to another.
From a life of sin to righteousness in Him
Through the precious blood of the Lamb
My life has been made over.
If any man is in Christ old things are past away
Jesus gave His life for us to have new life today
From the inside out we are renewed, our lives forever changed
His spirit lives within us because
My life has been made over, from one extreme to another.
From a life of sin to righteousness in Him
Through the precious blood of the Lamb
My life has been made over

Daily Reflections: *Your Thoughts on Today's Study*

Prayer Journal: *Your Prayer on Today's Study*

Appendix A: Dealing with the Past from A-Z

Dealing with the past from A-Z: 26 messages to help you deal with your past

A. I Corinthians 6:9-11: Know ye not that the unrighteous shall not inherit the kingdom of God? Be not deceived: neither fornicators, nor idolaters, nor adulterers, nor effeminate, nor abusers of themselves with mankind, [10]Nor thieves, nor covetous, nor drunkards, nor revilers, nor extortioners, shall inherit the kingdom of God. [11]And such were some of you: but ye are washed, but ye are sanctified, but ye are justified in the name of the Lord Jesus, and by the Spirit of our God.

B. Isaiah 43:18-19: Remember ye not the former things, neither consider the things of old. [19]Behold, I will do a new thing; now it shall spring forth; shall ye not know it? I will even make a way in the wilderness, and rivers in the desert.

C. Hebrews 10:16-17: This is the covenant that I will make with them after those days, saith the Lord, I will put my laws into their hearts, and in their minds will I write them; [17]And their sins and iniquities will I remember no more.

D. Luke 9:57-62: And it came to pass, that, as they went in the way, a certain man said unto him, Lord, I will follow thee whithersoever thou goest. [58]And Jesus said unto him, Foxes have holes, and birds of the air have nests; but the Son of man hath not where to lay his head. [59]And he said unto another, Follow me. But he said, Lord, suffer me first to go and bury my father. [60]Jesus said unto him, Let the dead bury their dead: but go thou and preach the kingdom of God. [61]And another also said, Lord, I will follow thee; but let me first go bid them farewell, which are at home at my house. [62]And Jesus said unto him, No man, having put his hand to the plow, and looking back, is fit for the kingdom of God.

E. Philippians 4:8: Finally, brethren, whatsoever things are true, whatsoever things are honest, whatsoever things are just, whatsoever things are pure, whatsoever things are lovely, whatsoever things are of good report; if there be any virtue, and if there be any praise, think on these things.

F. Romans 5:8-11: But God commendeth his love toward us, in that, while we were yet sinners, Christ died for us. [9]Much more then, being now justified by his blood, we shall be saved from wrath through him. [10]For if, when we were enemies, we were reconciled to God by the death of his Son, much more, being reconciled, we shall be saved by his life. [11]And not only so, but we also joy in God through our Lord Jesus Christ, by whom we have now received the atonement.

G. I Corinthians 10:13: There hath no temptation taken you but such as is common to man: but God is faithful, who will not suffer you to be tempted above that ye are able; but will with the temptation also make a way to escape, that ye may be able to bear it.

H. Micah 7:18-19: Who is a God like unto thee, that pardoneth iniquity, and passeth by the transgression of the remnant of his heritage? he retaineth not his anger for ever, because he delighteth in mercy. [19]He will turn again, he will have compassion upon us; he will subdue our iniquities; and thou wilt cast all their sins into the depths of the sea.

I. Jeremiah 31:33-34: But this shall be the covenant that I will make with the house of Israel; After those days, saith the LORD, I will put my law in their inward parts, and write it in their hearts; and will be their God, and they shall be my people. [34]And they shall teach no more every man his neighbour, and every man his brother, saying, Know the LORD: for they shall all know me, from the least of them unto the greatest of them, saith the LORD: for I will forgive their iniquity, and I will remember their sin no more.

J. I John 2:1-2: My little children, these things write I unto you, that ye sin not. And if any man sin, we have an advocate with the Father, Jesus Christ the righteous: [2]And he is the propitiation for our sins: and not for ours only, but also for the sins of the whole world.

K. Colossians 1:12-14: Giving thanks unto the Father, which hath made us meet to be partakers of the inheritance of the saints in light: [13]Who hath delivered us from the power of darkness, and hath translated us into the kingdom of his dear Son: [14]In whom we have redemption through his blood, even the forgiveness of sins:

L. Isaiah 44:22: I have blotted out, as a thick cloud, thy transgressions, and, as a cloud, thy sins: return unto me; for I have redeemed thee.

M. Ephesians 2:1-8: And you hath he quickened, who were dead in trespasses and sins; [2]Wherein in time past ye walked according to the course of this world, according to the prince of the power of the air, the spirit that now worketh in the children of disobedience: [3]Among whom also we all had our conversation in times past in the lusts of our flesh, fulfilling the desires of the flesh and of the mind; and were by nature the children of wrath, even as others. [4]But God, who is rich in mercy, for his great love wherewith he loved us, [5]Even when we were dead in sins, hath quickened us together with Christ, (by grace ye are saved;) [6]And hath raised us up together, and made us sit together in heavenly places in Christ Jesus: [7]That in the ages to come he might show the exceeding riches of his grace in his kindness toward us through Christ Jesus. [8]For by grace are ye saved through faith; and that not of yourselves: it is the gift of God:

N. I Corinthians 6:19-20: What? know ye not that your body is the temple of the Holy Ghost which is in you, which ye have of God, and ye are not your own? [20]For ye are bought with a price: therefore glorify God in your body, and in your spirit, which are God's.

O. Philippians 3:13-14: Brethren, I count not myself to have apprehended: but this one thing I do, forgetting those things which are behind, and reaching forth unto those things which are before, [14]I press toward the mark for the prize of the high calling of God in Christ Jesus.

P. Ephesians 4:22-23: That ye put off concerning the former conversation the old man, which is corrupt according to the deceitful lusts; [23]And be renewed in the spirit of your mind;

Q. Isaiah 43:25: I, even I, am he that blotteth out thy transgressions for mine own sake, and will not remember thy sins.

R. I John 1:9: If we confess our sins, he is faithful and just to forgive us our sins, and to cleanse us from all unrighteousness.

S. Colossians 1:21-22: And you, that were sometime alienated and enemies in your mind by wicked works, yet now hath he reconciled [22]In the body of his flesh through death, to present you holy and unblameable and unre-proveable in his sight:

T. Ephesians 5:8-11: For ye were sometimes darkness, but now are ye light in the Lord: walk as children of light: [9](For the fruit of the Spirit is in all goodness and righteousness and truth;) [10]Proving what is acceptable unto the Lord. [11]And have no fellowship with the unfruitful works of darkness, but rather reprove them.

U. Isaiah 55:6-9: Seek ye the LORD while he may be found, call ye upon him while he is near: [7]Let the wicked forsake his way, and the unright-eous man his thoughts: and let him return unto the LORD, and he will have mercy upon him; and to our God, for he will abundantly pardon. [8]For my thoughts are not your thoughts, neither are your ways my ways, saith the LORD. [9]For as the heavens are higher than the earth, so are my ways higher than your ways, and my thoughts than your thoughts.

V.   Isaiah 43:1: But now thus saith the LORD that created thee, O Jacob, and he that formed thee, O Israel, Fear not: for I have redeemed thee, I have called thee by thy name; thou art mine.

W.   Isaiah 54:4-8: Fear not; for thou shalt not be ashamed: neither be thou confounded; for thou shalt not be put to shame: for thou shalt forget the shame of thy youth, and shalt not remember the reproach of thy widowhood any more. ⁵For thy Maker is thine husband; the LORD of hosts is his name; and thy Redeemer the Holy One of Israel; The God of the whole earth shall he be called. ⁶For the LORD hath called thee as a woman forsaken and grieved in spirit, and a wife of youth, when thou wast refused, saith thy God. ⁷For a small moment have I forsaken thee; but with great mercies will I gather thee. ⁸In a little wrath I hid my face from thee for a moment; but with everlasting kindness will I have mercy on thee, saith the LORD thy Redeemer.

X.   Isaiah 40:28-31: Hast thou not known? hast thou not heard, that the everlasting God, the LORD, the Creator of the ends of the earth, fainteth not, neither is weary? there is no searching of his understanding. ²⁹He giveth power to the faint; and to them that have no might he increaseth strength. ³⁰Even the youths shall faint and be weary, and the young men shall utterly fall: ³¹But they that wait upon the LORD shall renew their strength; they shall mount up with wings as eagles; they shall run, and not be weary; and they shall walk, and not faint.

Y.   Colossians 2:13: And you, being dead in your sins and the uncircumcision of your flesh, hath he quickened together with him, having forgiven you all trespasses;

Z.   Colossians 3:2-3: Set your affection on things above, not on things on the earth. ³For ye are dead, and your life is hid with Christ in God.

Other books written by
Dr. Brenda J. Robinson

Seized For His Glory ....Dr. Robinson's Life Story

A New Desire ....365 day Daily Devotional

A New Desire Workbook ....Developing a personal Relationship with God
(A Six Week Bible Study)

A Victorious Christian Life ....Turning life's negatives into promising positives
(An Eight Week Bible Study)

It Is Finished ....Knowing where you stand with God

To order additional copies of

Made Over

Or other works by
Dr. Brenda J. Robinson
Please check your local Christian book store or
Call or Contact

New Desire Christian Ministries,Inc.
PO Box 918
Aragon, Ga 30104
770 684 8987
www.newdesire.org

Printed in the United States
69123LVS00002BB/151-500